Employee Engagement in Nonprofit Organizations

Kunle Akingbola · Sean Edmund Rogers ·
Melissa Intindola

Employee Engagement in Nonprofit Organizations

Theory and Practice

palgrave
macmillan

Kunle Akingbola
Lakehead University
Orillia, ON, Canada

Sean Edmund Rogers
University of Rhode Island
Kingston, RI, USA

Melissa Intindola
Freeman College of Management
Bucknell University
Lewisburg, PA, USA

ISBN 978-3-031-08468-3   ISBN 978-3-031-08469-0 (eBook)
https://doi.org/10.1007/978-3-031-08469-0

© The Editor(s) (if applicable) and The Author(s), under exclusive licence to Springer Nature Switzerland AG, part of Springer Nature 2023
This work is subject to copyright. All rights are solely and exclusively licensed by the Publisher, whether the whole or part of the material is concerned, specifically the rights of translation, reprinting, reuse of illustrations, recitation, broadcasting, reproduction on microfilms or in any other physical way, and transmission or information storage and retrieval, electronic adaptation, computer software, or by similar or dissimilar methodology now known or hereafter developed.
The use of general descriptive names, registered names, trademarks, service marks, etc. in this publication does not imply, even in the absence of a specific statement, that such names are exempt from the relevant protective laws and regulations and therefore free for general use.
The publisher, the authors, and the editors are safe to assume that the advice and information in this book are believed to be true and accurate at the date of publication. Neither the publisher nor the authors or the editors give a warranty, expressed or implied, with respect to the material contained herein or for any errors or omissions that may have been made. The publisher remains neutral with regard to jurisdictional claims in published maps and institutional affiliations.

This Palgrave Macmillan imprint is published by the registered company Springer Nature Switzerland AG
The registered company address is: Gewerbestrasse 11, 6330 Cham, Switzerland

Contents

1	Employee Engagement: What's the Deal?	1
2	Nonprofit Organizations: The Land of Engagement	37
3	Nonprofit Employee Engagement Model	77
4	Creating and Sustaining Employee Engagement Through Human Resource Management	95
5	Volunteer Engagement	119
6	Boards & Engagement: Spectrum of Involvement	141
7	Community Engagement: Beyond These Walls—Boards and Social Innovation via Advocacy	157
8	Measuring Engagement: Theoretical Perspectives and Practical Approaches	173
9	Huronia Transition Homes: Employee and Volunteer Engagement for Social Enterprise	191
Index		199

List of Figures

Fig. 1.1	Example of why employee engagement is a big deal	2
Fig. 1.2	Employee engagement concerns in manufacturing industry	11
Fig. 1.3	Employee engagement in hospitality industry	17
Fig. 1.4	Employee engagement and retention	26
Fig. 1.5	Proven ways for manufacturers to improve safety engagement and costs	27
Fig. 2.1	Nonprofit mission and values	39
Fig. 2.2	Adapting the mission	40
Fig. 2.3	New York cares adapt to community needs during COVID-19	44
Fig. 2.4	COVID-19 and nonprofit revenue in Canada	45
Fig. 2.5	COVID-19 and government funding	48
Fig. 2.6	Technology and nonprofit organizations	49
Fig. 2.7	Giving employees a voice	56
Fig. 3.1	Selander's extended JD-R model	83
Fig. 3.2	Akingbola and van den Berg's model of antecedents and consequences with organization and job engagement mediators	84
Fig. 3.3	Integrated nonprofit employee engagement model	86
Fig. 5.1	A simplified depiction of the Hackman et al. Job characteristics theory	128
Fig. 6.1	Continuum of involvement	146
Fig. 6.2	The Approach-engagement link	148
Fig. 7.1	Barriers to Advocacy	163

List of Tables

Table 2.1	Services of nonprofit organizations	42
Table 3.1	Employee supports and COVID-19 mitigation measures	78
Table 4.1	Enhancing employee engagement through human resource management and the creation of job resources	110
Table 5.1	Needs-based reasons for why people volunteer according to the volunteer functional inventory	122
Table 6.1	Three approaches to involvement	147
Table 8.1	Selected academic approaches to measuring employee engagement	176

CHAPTER 1

Employee Engagement: What's the Deal?

Employee engagement is a big deal. It is a big deal for employees and for organizations, Interestingly, employee engagement is also a big deal for society at large. It is a big deal from several angles and for multiple reasons all of which we will discuss and explain throughout this book. But suffice to say, employee engagement is such a big deal that it is worth examining not only as a positive organizational behavior construct but also as a continuously emergent behavioral state and process in organizations (see Fig. 1.1. Pandemic and Employee engagement). From the initial emergent of the construct of employee engagement in the 1990s to the early discourse of what it really means, and the questions about how it could shape employee and organizational outcomes and performance, the relevance and importance of employee engagement have been highlighted by the significant body of literature on the construct. Although the early uptake in the examination of employee engagement was spearheaded mostly in the management consulting literature, empirical research has followed suit to investigate, explain, and propose conceptual models. Now, we know more about what employee engagement means, its dimensions, and what difference it could make for employees and the organization.

With this background in mind, we introduce employee engagement. The chapter explains why employee engagement is such a big deal by discussing the basic notion of employee engagement. What does

> **PANDEMIC & EMPLOYEE ENGAGEMENT**
>
> One truth that the pandemic era has laid bare for businesses globally is that employees' emotional connection and engagement are inextricably linked to the overall health and function of a company's workforce, its ability to retain talent and, ultimately, to the company's success.
>
> Source: Micklethwait, J. (2022). Reimagining Employee Engagement in The Great Resignation Era. Forbes. Jun 8, 2022,06:00am EDT

Fig. 1.1 Example of why employee engagement is a big deal

employee engagement really mean? We provide an overview of the relevant definitions that have been suggested to explain the construct of employee engagement and the approaches used to explain employee engagement. To highlight how employee engagement is a multidimensional concept, we discuss how it is related to other organizational behavior concepts. Later in the chapter, we explain the benefits of employee engagement for the organization and the employees to highlight why it has become imperative for organizations.

Notion of Employee Engagement

A good way of starting the introduction to employee engagement is to explain what it is in simple terms. As a basic term that describes employee behaviors in organizations, one could suggest that the notion of employee engagement simply means dedication. Synonyms of dedication such as devotion and allegiance could also fit the bill when describing behaviors that characterize employee engagement. At its core, employee engagement is about dedication to the job. Employee engagement is about dedication to the tasks, processes, and the interactions that make up a job. In effect, what the job is about matters to the employee because of employee engagement. Similarly, employee engagement is about dedication to what the organization is all about. This means dedication to the mission that outlines the purpose, and the values that guide the activities, and decision-making in the organization. Importantly, employee engagement is about dedication to the performance of the organization. Employee engagement is such a big deal. It is the hallmark of the dedication of the employee.

The brief overview of the notion of employee engagement sets the tone for the in-depth discussion of the definitions and approaches used to explain the concept. The diverse but related explanation of the meaning of the employee behaviors that are indicative of employee engagement is essential to understand the ingredients that organizations must deploy to facilitate the achievement of the multidimensional impacts and outcomes for employees and the organization. The ingredients are also critical to develop and implement employee engagement plans that are aligned with the human resources strategy of the organization. Next, we explore the definitions of employee engagement based on three phases in the evolution of the concepts. Each phase highlights the emergent explanation of why employee engagement is a big deal.

Meaning of Employee Engagement

Employee engagement is a relatively new concept that has attracted diverse definitions in management consulting and academic literature. Perhaps, because employee engagement incorporates many existing concepts in human resource management and organizational behavior to explain what it means and how it impacts employees and the organization, the definitions of employee engagement tend to include more than one dimension (Macey & Schneider, 2008). Therefore, we present the definitions in three phases based on the evolving understanding of employee engagement.

Employee Engagement: Work Role Definitions

Kahn (1990) introduced the idea of engagement. Kahn defines engagement as "the simultaneous employment and expression of a person's 'preferred self' in task behaviors that promote connections to work and to others, personal presence (physical, cognitive, and emotional), and active, full role performances" (p. 700). This definition emphasizes that personal engagement is harnessing what the individual self has to offer in the work role. The definition describes how the individual is bringing the whole self that comprises the physical, cognitive, and emotional energy of the person to perform in their work roles. Kahn (1992) explained further that engagement is more than simple task motivation. Through engagement, the individual proves not only their commitment and buy-in in their work role, but they also express their true personal identity that helps to connect them to the job and address work issues (Macey & Schneider, 2008). Kahn's explanation of what employee engagement is connects the individual at a deeper personal level to the job.

The early days of employee engagement generated other relevant definitions that explain it as a motivational concept with additional elements. Maslach et al. (1996) define employee engagement as an energetic state in which employees are both dedicated to excellent performance and confident in their effectiveness. Their definition reinforced the connection of the self to the job by highlighting how employee engagement helps to take the employee away from a negative state of burnout. One research operationalized the concept of employee engagement with empirical measures and defined it "as a positive, fulfilling, work-related state of mind that is characterized by vigor, dedication, and absorption" (Schaufeli et al., 2002, p. 74). They clarified that

- Vigor means high levels of energy and willingness to invest effort in one's work.
- Dedication is about being deeply involved in one's work and experiencing a sense of significance, enthusiasm, inspiration, pride, and challenge.
- Absorption entails full concentration on one's work, to the point of experiencing time as passing quickly and difficulty in detaching oneself from work.

This means that employee engagement involves an ongoing and persistent state of mind that shows a disposition toward relentless effort, high level of energy, and drive for the job role (Schaufeli et al., 2002). It also includes affective behavior such as enthusiasm, attachment to the job, and the ability to overlook difficulties in the work role. In this definition, employee engagement includes presence of mind and an unencumbered focus on the job.

The work role definitions emphasize the connection of the employee to the job. They explain that employee engagement is a big deal because it means that employees are "truly into" the job because of the connection of the individual to the job beyond the basic psychological level.

These definitions explain the connection of the individual employee to the job by highlighting how employee engagement brings about positive psychological state—attitudes, emotions, and affective state—that feeds the energy and passion for the job. In sports analogy, one could say that the individual is bringing the best starting team with deep bench strength, and a winning attitude to the game.

Employee Engagement: Organizational Impacts Definitions

For a period, the work of management consultants led the way in highlighting the organizational impacts of employee engagement. This was particularly evidenced in their definition of employee engagement. They emphasized discretionary effort and the impacts of engagement on organizations. Towers Perrin defines employee engagement as the "employees' willingness and ability to help their company succeed, largely by providing discretionary effort on a sustainable basis" (Towers Perrin, 2003a). Their second report explained that employee engagement is "the extent to which employees put discretionary effort into their work, in the form of extra time, brainpower, and energy" (Towers Perrin, 2003b, p. 3). Gibbons (2006) defines employee engagement as the connection an employee has to their job, organization, manager, or coworkers, a connection that should lead to the application of additional discretionary effort in their work.

The discretionary effort narrative has been further simplified in subsequent reports by consultants, emphasizing the discretionary effort of employees to go beyond their job expectations (Caldwell, 2012; Towers Watson, 2014). The Towers Watson report noted that there are three measurable elements that are essential to sustainable employee engagement:

- Traditional employee engagement—employees' willingness to expend discretionary effort on their job.
- Enablement—having the tools, resources and support (typically through direct-line supervisors) to do their job effectively.
- Energy—having a work environment that actively supports physical, emotional and interpersonal well-being (Towers Watson, 2014, p. 3).

The definitions offered by management practitioners emphasize the connection of the employee to the job and how it impacts the organization. They suggest that employees rely on this connection to determine their level of employee engagement. The large body of survey reports by management consultants has also fostered the understanding of the basic premise of employee engagement. Until recently, much of the available management practitioner literature suggested definitions that link employee engagement to outcomes that are yet to be supported by research. However, it didn't take long before empirical research started to link employee engagement to organizational outcomes.

For Robinson et al. (2004), employee engagement is "a positive attitude held by the employee towards the organization and its values. An engaged employee is aware of the business context, works with colleagues to improve performance within the job for the benefit of the organization" (p. 2). From this standpoint, employee engagement is explained not only in terms of driving the relationship between the employee and the job but also to explain how the connection contributes to organizational outcomes. Although not a definition, Cartwright and Holmes (2006) explained that employee engagement impacts the need of employees to find meaning in their job and the productivity of the organization. In their analysis, employee engagement is part of the growing emphasis on intrinsic aspect of work that is characterized by a sense of meaning and purpose which benefits the outcomes of the organization.

The definitions that explain the impacts of employee engagement on organizational outcomes have become the dominant discourse among scholars who research employee engagement. Research has used this approach as the starting point for highlighting why employee engagement is a big deal. This perspective appears to have overtaken the original social-psychological definitions that emphasize the interaction of the individual and the work role. However, as discussed below, more recent definitions have taken a more comprehensive approach to explain what employee engagement is about. The most recent definitions have added to the line of research on the relationship between employee engagement, the individual, and the organization while raising questions about the nature of the construct.

Employee Engagement: Multidimensional Definitions

The evolution in the understanding of employee engagement has gained pace over a short period with emergent perspectives. This includes one distinct perspective that introduced a multidimensional approach to the definition of employee engagement. Saks (2006) defines employee engagement as "a distinct and unique construct consisting of cognitive, emotional, and behavioral components... associated with individual role performance" (p. 602). Saks explained that there is a difference between job engagement and organizational engagement. Job engagement is characterized by the degree to which the individual employees exert or invest the self in their work role, while organizational engagement could be conceptualized as the greater investment of the self for higher job performance in response to organizational factors or decisions (Saks, 2006). The key point in this definition is that there are different dimensions of employee engagement that may overlap. Employees can possibly be engaged through the characteristics and content of the job, that is the tasks, skills deployed to work on the job, and the social and psychological components of the job. At the same time, employees can also be engaged through organizational factors which include the mission, vision, and values as well as the interactions with people and processes of the organization. The organizational factors facilitate employee engagement simultaneously or separately from what the employee is required to do on the job.

Another angle in the multidimensional perspective explained that employee engagement is a concept that includes a composite of cognitive, emotional, and behavioral constructs (Swanberg et al., 2011). This approach extends the definition of employee engagement as "an individual employee's cognitive, emotional and behavioral state directed toward desired organizational outcomes" (Shuck & Wollard, 2010, p. 103). This suggests that engaged employees will demonstrate attentiveness and mental absorption in their work and at the same time, they will have a high level of emotional connection to the organization (Kahn, 1990; Saks, 2006). The link to organizational outcomes in this perspective suggests that employee engagement comes about because employees find meaningfulness in the outcomes of the organization. The multidimensional approach combines the elements of the work roles and organizational impacts perspectives to explain how the cognitive, emotional, and behavioral energies of employees are deployed for the benefit of the individual and the organization.

Employee Engagement: Team and Collective Organizational Engagement Definitions

One recent perspective has added a collective angle to the definition of employee engagement. It suggests that employee engagement does come about at a collective level. This could be at an organizational and/or team levels. Both types of collective employee engagement result in part from the social processes of the organization. This perspective explains that there is collective organizational employee engagement because employees do not only become engaged as individuals, but they can also be engaged collectively as a team or as members of the organization. Collective organizational engagement has been defined as the "shared perceptions of organizational members that members of the organization are, as a whole, physically, cognitively, and emotionally invested in their work" (Barrick et al., 2015, p. 113). Employee engagement is a product of the various organizational affective and social processes among employees through which they share perception and congruency of values. These interactions and processes ultimately contribute to shaping the characteristics of the organization including human resource management practices and job design.

Team engagement is the other dimension of the collective engagement perspective. Team engagement means that employees have shared perceptions. The team is seen as a unified whole, not a collection of separate individuals. Team engagement has been defined as "a positive, fulfilling, and shared emergent motivational state that is characterized by team vigor, team dedication, and team absorption, which emerges from the interactions and shared experiences of members of a team" (Costa et al., 2014, p. 35). Team engagement suggests that there is team cohesion and significant buy-in to the team norms among team members. For team engagement to manifest, there must be a convergence of behavioral factors not only among team members but also the leadership of the team. The synchronization of positive emotions that are related to work tasks, work activities, and work processes are good evidence that team engagement could be in play in an organization (Marks et al., 2001). Team engagement is signaling that team members connect at an emotional and affective state which plays a crucial role in directing their prosocial behavior such as organizational commitment. This helps team members to cooperate and share information. It is also an important building block for strong social bonding among team members.

What appears to make the collective engagement explanation unique is the idea of togetherness among members of the team and the organization. The similarity in behavioral state is about togetherness, which flows from the unity of purpose and values among members. This makes the team and the organization to find meaningfulness and achieve performance outcomes together. The degree of homogeneity, that is, similarity in the characteristics of employees is central to what makes collective organizational engagement and team engagement possible. The explanation sets the stage for a better understanding of employees who are collectively engaged at the team and organizational levels with the social processes of the organization as the foundation of engagement. Collective organizational and team engagement suggest that employees are engaged together, beyond their individual psychological experience. So, collective engagement is precipitated on the togetherness of the employees.

Doing Employee Engagement

Before we wrap up the meaning of employee engagement, it is relevant to acknowledge a new perspective that presents employee engagement as *management practice* (Truss et al., 2014). Unlike the existing conceptualizations that discuss the construct in terms of psychological state, the employee engagement as management practice perspective emphasizes practices that signal engagement such as employee involvement and participation. The focus of this HRM-centered perspective appears to be on practices that management deploys to facilitate employee engagement.

Synopsis: Mixed Bag of Employee Engagement

The perspectives that have been offered to explain and define employee engagement discussed above provide a good overview of our understanding of what employee engagement is all about. The perspectives highlight why employee engagement is a big deal in organizations. The *work role* explanation of employee engagement introduced us to how the psychological self connects to the job, that is, how we feel, think, and deploy our energy in relations to the collections of tasks or duties that make up our job. The *organizational impact* definitions of employee engagement are centered on how the discretionary effort of employees that results from employee engagement impacts the outcomes of the organization. From the organizational impact perspective, employee engagement means that the employee finds the job to be meaningful and has a decent working relationship with their manager and colleagues. Together, this enhances the performance of the organization. The *multidimensional definitions* add a distinct explanation that differentiates job engagement and organizational engagement. Although the relationship between the employee and the job on the one hand, and their relationship with the organization on the other hand, are explained as different dimensions of employee engagement, the two are intertwined. Job characteristics including tasks and skills variety are connected to and influenced by organizational factors, interactions, and processes. *Collective employee engagement* added that employees do become engaged collectively, that is, together as a unit at the organizational and/or team levels. The collective explanation focuses on shared experience of employee engagement within the organization.

In all, the definitions highlight that employee engagement is a big deal. Employee engagement is a big deal because it is a composite and integrative explanation of how the simultaneous expression of individual cognitive, emotional, and behavioral energies, the individual experience of organizational factors, and the collective shared social processes drive individual and organizational outcomes. The diverse but highly interrelated explanations of employee engagement suggest that the construct is about the individual and collective meaningfulness that employees experience in organizations. The employee engagement concerns in the manufacturing industry illustrate why organizations need to take employee engagement seriously (Fig. 1.2).

APPROACHES TO EMPLOYEE ENGAGEMENT

The question of what employee engagement is all about could also be explained through the lens of approaches that researchers have used to explain the construct. While the definitions that introduce the meaning of employee engagement are upshot of many of the major perspectives that researchers and practitioners have offered to define what being engaged really looks and feels like, the broad approaches to employee engagement give us an idea of what the proponents were thinking

> **Engagement in Manufacturing Industry**
>
> According to a report by Gallup, manufacturing employees are the least engaged of all fields surveyed, with only 25 percent saying they feel engaged at work. Common engagement tactics such as company-wide emails, individual events, or the occasional award won't produce strong results on their own. In order to see real change, businesses need to go deeper to truly address sticking points within their company culture.
>
> Sztutwojner, D. (2020). 4 Ways to Fix Manufacturing's Employee Engagement Problem. https://www.manufacturing.net/operations/blog/21140191/4-ways-to-fix-manufacturings-employee-engagement-problem

Fig. 1.2 Employee engagement concerns in manufacturing industry

when they postulated the idea of employee engagement. Therefore, the approaches to employee engagement are another worthwhile way of further explaining employee engagement. We suggest that there are five approaches that have been offered that also highlight the explanation of employee engagement: (a) Employee engagement as motivation; (b) Employee engagement as satisfaction; (c) Employee engagement as commitment; (d) Employee engagement as job resources; (e) Employee engagement as shared values.

Employee Engagement as a Motivational Mechanism

From the early introduction of the idea of employee engagement (Kahn, 1990) to more recent conceptualization, the construct has been explained as a mechanism for motivation. Employee engagement is conceived of as the deployment of the personal self in terms of the physical, cognitive, and emotional energy in the performance of work roles (Kahn, 1990). Employee engagement is like a tonic that fuels the energy to use a varying amount of the employee's self to do their job at a higher level of performance. It is more than showing up and being psychologically present at work (Kahn, 1992). Rather, employee engagement behaviors include deeper connection with the work roles to address challenging issues, doing work differently as well as fostering positive working relationships.

The motivational mechanism explanation of employee engagement in subsequent research has further emphasized how it drives positive work-related behaviors and state of mind. Schaufeli et al. (2002) noted that the positive behaviors are characterized by vigor, dedication, and absorption. Employee engagement makes these individual and organizational desirable types of behaviors possible for employees because they are fully clued into their job and the organization. Employee engagement drives employees to exercise perseverance, be more flexible, and eagerly seek ways to solve work-related problems (Zhang & Bartol, 2010). The energy of employee engagement also drives the positive emotional labor between employees and their supervisors (Wu & Wu, 2019). In a way, this research is saying that the manager and their subordinates can withstand each other. They can endure the tension built into their professional and interpersonal interaction.

What the employee engagement as motivational mechanism explanation is highlighting is that the construct is a driver or factor in the expression of motivation. As a mechanism, it means that employee engagement facilitates or makes it possible for the motivation to deploy the behaviors and state of mind. In the language of modern social media, employee engagement is like an influencer. They make employees do the things that they prefer and benefit the organization.

Employee Engagement as Satisfaction

The understanding of the meaning of employee engagement often includes a dimension of its explanation as satisfaction. Perhaps, satisfaction plus is a better way of describing this explanation because it does not suggest that employee engagement is simply the same as satisfaction. Rather, employee engagement is explained to include the feeling of satisfaction (Macey & Schneider, 2008). The internal mental state characterized by the feeling of satisfaction that employees experience when they are engaged is a particularly relevant way to clarify the confusion about the nature of employee engagement. This feeling of satisfaction that employees experience in conjunction with the behavior in turn play a role in determining their experience of employee engagement.

The point about explaining employee engagement as satisfaction has evolved from research that attempts to broaden our understanding of the concept while providing empirical evidence of the relationship between the two constructs. In this light, studies have indicated that job satisfaction is an antecedent (Shuck & Wollard, 2010) and is a major predictor of employee engagement. It has also been suggested that there is an indirect relationship between the two constructs because satisfaction is a mediator in the relationship between antecedents and the outcomes (Rich et al., 2010).

The different findings suggest three key points about the relationship between satisfaction and employee engagement. One, satisfaction is associated with employee engagement. This could mean employees who have job satisfaction are more likely to be engaged than others. Two, the findings also appear to suggest that the relationship between antecedents and job satisfaction could depend on employee engagement as a mediating factor. Three, the literature has indicated that employee engagement appears not to predict job satisfaction which suggests that the relationship between the two constructs may not be vice-versa.

Employee Engagement as Commitment

Commitment is another well-known construct that has inevitably been prominent in the explanation of employee engagement. Commitment is conceived to be similar to employee engagement because both are a binding force (Macey & Schneider, 2008). The two concepts explain a type of connection that is akin to a psychological bond and sense of social identity that employees develop and deploy in organizations. Employee engagement and commitment explain the power of the connection between the employee and the job tasks as well as the relationship between the employee and the organization including their supervisor and team members. Although the constructs overlap, the literature has consistently explained that commitment is embedded in employee engagement (Shuck & Wollard, 2010). Employee engagement is more of a big umbrella construct that includes commitment.

As commitment, employee engagement means employees are willing to go beyond the routine job requirements. They have significant buy-in to what their job is about and derive a sense of identity from their job and membership in the organization (Bakker & Schaufeli, 2008). Employee engagement explained in terms of commitment means a positive psychological state characterized by dedication to the job, dedication to address challenging issues, dedication to stand up for and to represent the organization even in times of crisis. This notion of employee engagement was evidenced in an early definition of the concept *as an energetic state in which employees are both dedicated to excellent performance and confident in their effectiveness* (Maslach et al., 1996). It is about dedication to take on responsibility for and to deploy energy in the performance of the tasks for the organization (Klein et al., 2012). Employees exemplify commitment when they deploy behaviors that are consistent with attachment, bonding, and belongingness (Mowday et al., 1982). Employee engagement as commitment is indicative of a deep relationship between the employee and the organization.

Employee Engagement as Job Resources

The job resources explanation is one of the emergent perspectives in the discourse of employee engagement. It is based on the job demands and resources (JD-R) model, widely used in engagement research. Job resources are the key physical, social, or organizational aspects of the job that are critical for the employee to achieve work-related goals, to reduce demands and the associated costs, and to stimulate personal growth and development (Bakker & Demerouti, 2007). Specific examples of job resources include job autonomy, support, training, support for development, and supervisory coaching (Bakker & Bal, 2010). Central to job resources is that they are within the control of the employer, that is, the organization. They are resources that the organization facilitates or provides and can leverage in their relationship with employees (Newton, 2015). Job resources are important in shaping overall employee well-being and their performance on the job. In addition to facilitating the cognitive and emotional well-being of employees, job resources can play a role in driving the intrinsic or extrinsic motivation of employees. At the intrinsic level of motivation, they help to meet the human needs of employees in terms of autonomy, relatedness, and competence (Bakker & Bal, 2010, p. 191). Thus, job resources are important to the organization as they are to the employee.

It is in this vein that employee engagement has been explained in terms of job resources. Employees bring their personal resources, which are basically their individual characteristics, to the job. Examples of personal characteristics include attitude, personality, behavior and lived experiences. The personal characteristics of employees respond to, are impacted by, and impact the demands of the job. The combination of individual resources and job resources with job demands mediating the relationship, foster employee engagement (Bakker & Demerouti, 2007; Newton, 2015). Job resources are particularly related to employee engagement. Studies have suggested that all the six job resources; job control, supervisor support, climate, innovativeness, information, and appreciation, that were examined in empirical research, have a positive relationship with the core dimensions of employee engagement (Demerouti et al., 2001). The research found that vigor, dedication, and absorption which characterize employee engagement (Schaufeli et al., 2002), were positively related to employee engagement. In other words, employees who have a positive perception of their experience of the six job resources are more likely to deploy a high level of energy and enthusiasm about their work role and the organization. They are also likely to be keenly connected and engrossed in their job.

Perhaps the most important point is that employee engagement is played out through job resources when employees experience appreciation (Bakker et al., 2007, p. 279). When employees have a positive perception of how the organization deploys and uses their job resources including learning and autonomy, employee engagement is likely to result. This, in turn, benefits organizational outcomes (Gorgievski & Hobfoll, 2008). The employee perception of the job resources that the organization controls and how they are leveraged are not only relevant but important explanation of what employee engagement is all about. Job resources are antecedents that are at the core of employee engagement.

Employee Engagement as Shared Values

The notion of employee engagement as shared values is the newest of the emergent explanation of what employee engagement is about. In fact, it could be argued that this explanation is still in fragments and is yet to become a concise description of employee engagement. Shared values are values, principles, norms, beliefs, and practices that are espoused and commonly adopted by employees and the leadership of an organization (McDonald & Gandz, 1992). Shared values result from the core values of the organization, the culture, systems, and processes that the leadership put in place, interactions among employees, and their relationship with managers in the organization. Shared values contribute to individual employee outcomes including performance, well-being, and turnover (Lages et al., 2020; Watrous et al., 2006). It fosters team cohesion and outcomes, and the competitive advantage of the organization (Amah & Ahiauzu, 2014; Baltzley, 2016; Okafor, 2008). Shared values mean connection among employees based on commonly endorsed guiding principles and philosophies.

Shared values have consequences for the level of employee engagement through many mechanisms, some of which are related to team engagement (Costa et al., 2014). First, as employee engagement, shared values describe a building block for a workplace community that is created through the deliberate development and implementation of specific organizational culture and practices that create a congruence of meaning among employees. Collective engagement can therefore result from specific design and deployment of inputs such as job design, organizational structure, and type of leadership behavior (Costa et al., 2014). The substance of these organizational components has implications for employee engagement and team processes.

Second, the building block for the workplace community that facilitates employee engagement could also come about organically in that the shared meaning results from the social interactions and processes in the organization. The quality of interpersonal processes, that is, how employees address conflict with colleagues, and motivate each other, as well as whether they are aware of and respond to the affect of each other, could impact the level of employee engagement. Affect is a term in psychology that refers to any form of experience of emotion or feeling which could vary from simple to complex based on duration, intensity, etc. (Niven, 2013). The affective state is a core component of the social interactions in organizations that could impact the level of employee engagement.

Third, for individual employees, the convergence of values with other employees could be due to emotional contagion (Hatfield et al., 1994). This occurs through the transmittal of nonverbal codes of emotions such as tone of voice and facial expression, which are subconsciously adopted and replicated by other individuals resulting in similar experience of emotions (Costa et al., 2014). Employees copy and unknowingly experience the emotions first displayed by others. Emotional contagion facilitates employee engagement because employees perceive, observe, and replicate the emotions or feelings of their colleagues. The similarity contributes to the experience of employee engagement among team members.

Fourth, convergence of values is also possible when employees have similar perceptions of an emergent psychological state such as motivation. A significant level of similar perceptions of the psychological state would ensure that employees can transcend their individual perceptions which would foster collective employee engagement. A high level of variability in perceptions could limit collective employee engagement because it reduces the opportunity to align values among employees and enhance the focus on individual perceptions (Fig. 1.3).

Whichever way it emerges, shared values connect employees as team members and as colleagues in the organization. Ultimately, the organizational environment provides the channel through which employees' shared values bring about employee engagement. Shared values manifest into employee engagement through the social resources of the organization such as a supportive organizational climate which enhance the opportunities for the sharing of meaningfulness, high motivational levels, and contribute to employee engagement.

The experience of employee engagement as shared values. as job resources, as commitment, as satisfaction, or as motivational mechanism highlight approaches that have been used to explain, understand, and empirically test the relationship between employee engagement and relevant social and psychological factors. These approaches have also provided insight into the factors that contribute to the level of employee engagement, both for individuals, teams, and at the collective organizational level.

How Employee Engagement Works in the Hospitality Industry.

Aligning employees' goals with your Engaged Purpose is the first step to giving your staff what they need to deliver unforgettable experiences (that result in outstanding reviews and increased bookings).

Source: How Employee Engagement Works in the Hospitality Industry. https://www.engagementmultiplier.com/resources/engaged-employees-happy-guests-how-employee-engagement-works-in-the-hospitality-industry/

Fig. 1.3 Employee engagement in hospitality industry

Antecedents of Employee Engagement

The definitions and the relevant explanations of why employee engagement is such a big deal generally include explicit and implicit pointers about the diverse factors or drivers that foster employee engagement. Research has examined many factors that are antecedents of the level of employee engagement and underlie the employee's experience of employee engagement. It is important to note that while the extensive list of antecedents is diverse, they overlap. Drawing from employee engagement research, this section provides an overview of the numerous antecedents of employee engagement (see Barrick et al., 2015; May et al., 2004; Newton, 2015; Schmidt, 2009). It highlights the factors or drivers based on three categories: (a) employee antecedents; (b) organizational antecedents; and (c) leadership antecedents.

Employee antecedents are factors that are specific to individual employees. The factors are related to the internal emotional and cognitive states of employees as well as their job role, and their interactions with team members and the organization. Research has suggested that many of the individual antecedents fall within the category of employee perception of working conditions (Crawford et al., 2010). Some examples of employee antecedents are:

- *Clear goals.* A clearly defined purpose of the job of the employee, its role in relation to the mission of the organization, and how it is connected to other jobs are relevant to facilitate employee engagement.
- *Challenging work.* The job of the employee must be relatively challenging to induce the deployment of emotional, cognitive, and behavioral energy required for job performance. When employees find the job challenging, they want to invest the *self* in the tasks of the job.
- *Autonomy.* Employees need to have appropriate decision-making authority on the job to be engaged. At a minimum, having a say in how they perform the tasks in their job contribute to employee engagement.
- *Customer satisfaction.* The feedback that employees experience through customer satisfaction contribute to their employee engagement.

- *Teamwork experience.* The shared perception that employees experience in teams contributes to their level of employee engagement. Also, it is not uncommon for employees to feed off the positive or negative vibes from their colleagues which impacts employee engagement.
- *Career opportunities.* Employees develop the perception of support when the organization offers career opportunities. This fosters employee engagement because employees develop a perception to invest the self in the organization.
- *Rewards and recognition.* Employees deploy discretion efforts based on their perception of the value the organization attaches to their work role and their performance. Rewards and recognition contribute to employee engagement at the individual employee and collective organizational levels.
- *Perceptions of trust in the organization.* This facilitates employee engagement through the process of social exchange. Employees develop a duty to reciprocate when they have the perception that the organization trusts them.
- *Empowerment.* The opportunity to improve one's work fosters employee engagement. Employees are likely to deploy more of their discretional efforts when the organization provides the opportunity, resources, and decision-making leeway to improve their work.
- *Equity and fairness.* The perception of fairness and equity in the policies and practices of the organization contribute to the level of employee engagement of employees. At all levels of the organization, employees' perception of fairness and equity play into their employee engagement.

Organizational antecedents. Generally, organizations have significant resources and opportunities to facilitate employee engagement. Although many of the employee antecedents overlap with organizational factors or drivers, the organizational antecedents are distinct factors that are tied to the resources that are controlled by the organization. The antecedents are also possible challenges that only the organization can address. Organizations typically have discretion in terms of how they deploy the resources they provide or how they decide to address the challenges. Examples of organizational antecedents are:

- *Job design.* The way tasks are combined to make up a job, the interdependence between jobs, the human, and the technical components of the job design are all important to foster employee engagement. Organizations can design jobs that employees will find fulfilling and have significant autonomy while performing the tasks and activities related to the job. Employees are better able to apply the self and invest their physical, emotional, and cognitive energy when organizations design jobs to match the competency, social, and psychological needs of the employees. Motivating job design play an important role in employee engagement.
- *Employee participation.* The degree to which employees have opportunities to participate in decision-making about their job, provide feedback to managers and senior leadership, and to engage in meaningful dialogue about the policies and strategy of the organization is a core component of job resources. These management practices are part of job resources which are performance levers or strategies available to organizations to deploy. When the organization seeks input from employees, it opens the door for an enhanced level of employee engagement. Employee perception of meaningfulness of their job and their psychological safety—sense of support and freedom to do the job without fear of negative consequence (Kahn, 1990)—contribute to employee engagement.
- *Commitment to employee well-being.* The organization must implicitly and explicitly be committed to the well-being of employees to foster employee engagement. The espoused and sincere interest of senior leadership in employee well-being could enhance how employees experience psychological safety which is a necessary condition for the investment of the self and psychological resources in the performance of the job. In other words, when employees know that the organization has their back, they are more likely to go the extra mile for the organization.
- *Adequate resources.* Employees must have the resources they need to perform their jobs. In a way, this could be the baseline for job resources to facilitate employee engagement because the inability to provide adequate resources means higher level job resources related to policies and practices are secondary. By providing adequate quality resources that employees require to perform their jobs, the organization is enabling a positive perception of the importance of the jobs

of the employees. Thus, the organization is setting up the stage for psychological meaningfulness that fosters employee engagement.

Leadership antecedents. Leadership is evidently a factor in both employee and organizational antecedents. Leaders play a critical role in providing an enabling environment for the personal resources of employees to flourish in their job roles and work-related interactions. Leaders are primarily responsible for developing, implementing, and evaluating the use and effectiveness of the job resources that constitute organizational antecedents. Beyond their central role in facilitating employee and organizational antecedents, the behavior of leaders are important antecedents of employee engagement (Bailey et al., 2017). There is consensus among researchers that transformational leadership may increase the level of employee engagement in organizations (Bakker et al., 2006). Transformational leadership is a type of leadership that; (i) develops and communicates an inspiring vision; (ii) models or exemplifies the vision; (iii) encourages and motivates experimentation; and (iv) facilities and builds commitment to the vision. We highlight three examples of leadership antecedents below.

Vision and shared values. The vision that encapsulates the inspirational purpose of the organization is an important tool for leaders to facilitate employee engagement. By embracing visionary leadership, the senior leaders in the organization can influence how employees experience meaningfulness which is critical for employee engagement (Piccolo & Colquitt, 2006; Podolny et al., 2005). Leaders do this by ensuring that the core values of the organization permeate job design, policies, and practices that they implement (Bakker, 2011). Senior leadership must work to create and sustain an organizational culture that fosters the shared values important to facilitate the positive attitude and behavior that characterize employee engagement.

Problem solver. Leadership has the responsibility to address the challenges that hinder employees from experiencing employee engagement (Pratt & Ashforth, 2003). The meaningfulness they aim to actualize is part of their role as problem solvers who are tasked with removing the barriers to create the necessary conditions for employee engagement. Consistent with path-goal leadership, this responsibility of the leaders is all about making work and the workplace meaningful for employees (House, 1997; Michaelson et al., 2014). They motivate by managing the expectancies of employees related job resources that are central to psychological safety. In effect, leadership ensures that the focus of employees is not distracted by problems that are within the control of the organization.

Communication and implementation. The task of effectively communicating organizational initiatives is one of the primary responsibilities of leaders. Communication involves leaders clearly articulating the vision, the values, and the implementation of the policies and practices of the organization. Communication about the vision and values of the organization is central to facilitating employee engagement. Information must flow with transparency and should be both downward from the senior leadership and upward from the frontline and operational units of the organization to promote employee engagement. The role of communication is especially heightened during a crisis when how problems and issues are communicated and managed carry existential consequences for the organization (Hicks, 2011). Leaders build trust by giving employees a voice and listening to their inputs in the communication process. Trust in leadership is a fundamental step for employee engagement both at the individual and collective levels in the organization (Cartwright & Holmes, 2006). Employees want to know that the senior leadership cares about their well-being and understands the issues that matter to them. This is what employees expect from transformational leadership and it is key to their role in fostering employee engagement.

The antecedents of employee engagement provide an important roadmap for the understanding of why and how employees experience employee engagement. Employee, organizational, and leadership antecedents are central to fostering the necessary conditions for employee engagement. Employee antecedents highlight the role of personal and job resources while organizational antecedents highlight how the drivers within the control of the organizations contribute to the level of employee engagement. Leadership antecedents are critical in any organization that aims to create enabling environment for employee engagement.

Benefits of Employee Engagement

Based on our proposition that employee engagement is a big deal, the logical question is, what is really in employee engagement for anyone? and what are the benefits of employee engagement for the organization? First, we need to acknowledge that embedded in each of the definitions and approaches that have explained employee engagement, are the numerous benefits of the psychological state and the process of engagement that employees experience. In addition, the antecedents of employee engagement discussed above provide more insights and dimensions on the benefits of employee engagement. Beyond the scattered references to the benefits of the construct, the section below provides an overview of what individuals, teams, and organizations, stand to gain from the level of engagement that employees experience.

Employee Engagement: What is in it for employees

For individuals, research has highlighted several benefits that accrue to employees from employee engagement (Pitt-Catsouphes & Matz-Costa, 2008). Although the benefits from research findings are about individual employees, they are also related to outcomes that benefit the organization and society at large. Here are some of what employees stand to gain from employee engagement.

Meaningfulness. Engaged employees are more likely to experience fulfillment and meaningfulness at a deeply personal level. The state and process of employee engagement that employees experience contribute to their perception of fulfillment. What comes with meaningfulness such as deep satisfaction and perception of individual contribution is such a big deal that employees have rated these intrinsic factors as more important to them than money. "People rate purpose, fulfillment, autonomy, satisfaction, close working relationships and learning as more important than money" (Cartwright & Holmes, 2006, p. 200). The experience of meaningfulness is shaped by the context of the organization, what employees do, and the people they work with.

Well-being. Employee experience of employee engagement plays an important role in their well-being within and outside of the organization. In addition to enhancing their level of satisfaction, employee engagement reinvigorates their career aspiration by building on their self-concept. This frees up their mind and self-confidence to participate in organizational activities that are not required in their job role (Parker & Martin, 2009). Employees develop the perception that the workplace is a safe space where they are free to experiment and relate with colleagues with no apprehension about potential risks. They come to work knowing that they are contributing to the organization in a meaningful way which enhances their well-being in terms of job, work interactions, and the organization.

Quality of work life. The impacts of employee engagement in terms of psychological meaningfulness, safety, and availability are relevant means for enhancing the quality of work life of employees. Early research linked the level of employee engagement to the enhanced quality of experience at work, that is opportunity to derive a better experience from their work life than others who are not engaged (Kahn, 1992). The work becomes less onerous because employee quality of work life is supported by the organizational environment.

Antidote against burnout. In a way, employee engagement means no or less burnout for employees. Early research indicates that employee engagement contributes to the ability of the employee to mitigate the negative state of burnout (Maslach et al., 1996). The link to burnout demonstrated that employee engagement is inversely related to a negative psychological outcome of the job for the employee. Burnout is essentially a health impairment that manifests when the job resources in the organization is inadequate for the demands of the job (Schaufeli & Bakker, 2004). In other words, a health impairment that impacts employee engagement.

Positive emotions. The opportunity to experience positive emotions has been suggested to be fundamental to understanding how people flourish (Fredrickson, 2001). People like to be happy and when they are happy, they flourish. The attitudes and behavior that flow from positive emotions are desirable to employees (Bakker & Schaufeli, 2008). Along this line, employee engagement is a desirable emotional experience for employees because it allows the employee to access positive emotions. Employees who are engaged have a better shot at experiencing positive emotions (Yalabik et al., 2013). When engaged employees experience positive emotions such as "happiness, joy, and enthusiasm; experience better health, they create their own job and personal resources; and transfer their employee engagement to others" (Bakker & Demerouti, 2008, p. 215). This impact of employee engagement on employees highlights an important individual outcome that contributes to employee performance and well-being.

Employee Engagement: What is in it for organizations

It goes without saying that all the benefits of employee engagement to employees directly and indirectly work to the advantage of the organization. Employee behavior, attitudes, and emotions are intrinsically related to employee outcomes. But beyond what is derived from the benefits to employees, organizations stand to gain quite a lot of benefits from employee engagement. In fact, a significant body of research and management literature has been devoted to understanding the benefits of employee engagement to organizations. Below, we discuss an overview of the major benefits that organizations can derive from employee engagement.

Productivity. Perhaps the top consequence of employee engagement for organizations that have been highlighted in the literature is the impact on productivity and profit. Employee engagement has a positive relationship with productivity and profitability (Bakker & Schaufeli, 2008; Harter et al., 2002). Employees deploy their cognitive, emotional, and behavioral energy at a higher level which results in increased productivity. The higher productivity that is associated with employee engagement is an upshot of the benefits to engaged employees coupled with organizational and leadership factors. Employee engagement means that employees are sufficiently engaged with the context of the organization which contributes to their level of productivity.

Profit. The impact of employee engagement on employee productivity often translates into higher profitability in for-profit business organizations. Research indicates that there is a relationship between business unit profit and employee engagement as well as overall corporate profitability (Harter et al., 2002; Luthans & Peterson, 2002). Moreover, the impact of employee engagement is also related to relevant organizational outcomes that underlie profitability such as product quality, better cost control, and financial performance (Towers Perrin, 2003a). The findings on the positive relationship between employee engagement and profitability are consistent in the literature. Thus, there appears to be a consensus among researchers that when employees are engaged, it bodes well for the profitability of the organization.

Turnover. Employee turnover is one of the individual outcomes that have direct implications for the organization. Research has repeatedly indicated that decreased employee turnover is related to employee engagement (Crawford et al., 2010; Shuck et al., 2011). Also, a similar relationship between employee engagement and employee turnover intention in the organization has been suggested in the findings of several studies (Saks, 2006; Shuck et al., 2011; Shuck & Wollard, 2010). Although both have a negative relationship with employee engagement, employee turnover, and turnover intention have similar consequences for the organization. High employee turnover and turnover intention affect productivity, morale, and job satisfaction. However, turnover has implications for the cost of recruitment, training, and loss of organizational or institutional memory. Turnover intention could have the additional consequence of contributing to a toxic environment in the organizations. Since turnover intention is a predictor of actual turnover (Steel & Ovalle, 1984), the difference in the consequences is less important. Employee engagement is associated with turnover. Employee engagement is a process that could help the organization to address the challenges of turnover and turnover intention (Fig. 1.4).

Change and innovation. Engaged employees are more likely to be ready to adapt to change than other employees. The positive behavior and emotions of engaged employees means that the organization has a committed pool of employees who are dedicated and have positive change readiness. Research has reiterated this position by highlighting that cognitive, emotional, and behavioral energy of employees could have an impact on change in organizations (Reissner & Pagan, 2013). In effect, employee engagement could play an important role in organizational change. Employee engagement equips employees with the necessary positive psychological state and behavior that are required for effective change management. The role of employee engagement is also important in enhancing organizational capacity for innovation (Bakker & Demerouti, 2008). Engaged employees facilitate and support innovation in the organization because they are more willing to deploy their discretionary effort.

Organizational citizenship, accidents, and safety. Engaged employees are more likely to use organizational citizenship behaviors such as taking on additional tasks voluntarily, exercising civic virtue, and helping colleagues on the job (Rich et al., 2010; Shuck & Wollard, 2010). This

---

Employee Engagement & Retention

"In terms of predicting performance, engagement is more important than retention, in my experience".

Source: Roley, R. (2020). Five Tips To Boost Employee Engagement In The Finance Industry> Forbes. April, 2020.https://www.forbes.com/sites/forbesfinancecouncil/2020/04/08/five-tips-to-boost-employee-engagement-in-the-finance-industry/?sh=7006136a3af2

Fig. 1.4 Employee engagement and retention

suggests that organizational citizenship behaviors foster the positive environment factors that are necessary for job and organizational performance (LePine et al., 2002). The organization benefits at the corporate and team levels from the impacts of organizational citizenship behavior (Saks, 2006). Similarly, the organization benefits from the decreased rate of accidents that is associated with the level of employee engagement. In other words, employee engagement contributes to behaviors that promote safety in the organization (Fig. 1.5).

Customer Satisfaction. The need to meet customer expectations is fundamental to organizations irrespective of size and type of business. Therefore, it cannot be overemphasized that customer satisfaction is a core organizational outcome. Organizations devote resources to facilitate, support, and sustain customer satisfaction. The experience of customer satisfaction can be defined as the degree of happiness that customers derive when they access or use the products, services, and capabilities of the organization. The relationship between employees and customers is a two-way street. On the one hand, employees play an important role in customer satisfaction. The quality of customer service that employees provides is central to the experience of customers. On the other hand, customer satisfaction contributes to employee engagement. Employees receive feedback through customer satisfaction, this contributes to their

---

Proven Ways for Manufacturers to Improve Safety Engagement and Costs

- Safety starts at the top: Understanding leadership's role
- Creating a strong safety culture
- Building ownership of safety using robust metrics
- Achieving employee engagement
- Implementing a Safety Management System (SMS)

Source: Goulart, C (2020). Proven Ways for Manufacturers to Improve Safety Engagement and Costs
https://www.manufacturing.net/home/article/21119796/proven-practices-for-distributors-to-improve-employee-engagement-drive-down-costs-and-elevate-safety

---

Fig. 1.5 Proven ways for manufacturers to improve safety engagement and costs

level of employee engagement. Research suggests that employee engagement mediates the relationship between job resources and service climate (Salanova et al., 2005). Employee engagement contributes to service climate, that is, how employees relate to customers and ultimately, to customer loyalty.

Employee Disengagement

One could simply assume that disengagement is the opposite of employee engagement. As a result, by extension, employees who are not engaged are disengaged. Without going into the debate on that line of thinking, we take the position that disengagement is simply a separate psychological state with distinct factors that are related to employee engagement. Disengagement has been defined "as the decoupling of the self from the work role and involves people withdrawing and defending themselves during role performances" (May et al., 2004, p. 12). It is characterized by employees who have literally tuned out of the job and the organization. They are disinterested and demotivated to perform their job and unwilling to participate in job-related activities.

Many of the same factors that contribute to the level of employee engagement are relevant in activating disengagement. For example, perceived lack of equity and fairness could bring about disengagement (Maslach & Leiter, 2008). Employees interpret their experience with the policies and practices of the organization to develop their perception of equity and fairness which, if negative, may contribute to employee disengagement. Similarly, lack of autonomy on the job is an important factor that could contribute to disengagement (Luthans & Peterson, 2002). The perception that there is a lack of meaningfulness may result in disengagement.

The consequences of disengagement are potentially extensive and particularly damaging to the organization. Employees who are disengaged are less likely to be productive which can affect the performance of the organization. Also, through emotional contagion, the behaviors of disengaged employees may affect the level of employee engagement of their coworkers. During organizational change, research suggests that disengaged employees are more likely to have negative attitudes about change (Vakola & Nikolaou, 2005). Disengaged employees can limit change readiness and impact how the change is perceived positively by employees in the organization.

CONCLUSION

Our foremost goal in this chapter is to explain why employee engagement is truly a big deal. In doing so, we drew on the continuously growing body of research to introduce the notion of employee engagement. We note that the notion of employee engagement is a good starting point to explain what it is in simple terms. The meaning of employee engagement is a mixed bag that incorporates perspectives that have been offered to explain and define the construct. The lens on the approaches that researchers have used to explain the construct offer insights into their thought process and the linkage between employee engagement and other relevant organizational behavior constructs. Engaged employees deploy their cognitive, emotional, and behavioral energy for outcomes that benefit the employees and the organization. With the antecedents like an inducer, employee engagement is facilitated through processes that involve personal, job, and organizational resources. It motivates the employees to invest the self in productive work, interactions, and work activities that they deem and find challenging and rewarding for them and the organization.

WHAT'S NEXT

This book explores the theory and practice of employee engagement in nonprofit organizations. It draws on research to examine the antecedents, dimensions, and consequences of employee engagement in nonprofit organizations. The book provides evidence-based context-specific models for the deployment of employee engagement to facilitate how individuals and teams contribute to and enhance organizational performance and community outcomes in nonprofit organizations. The experience of meaningful work that underlies employee engagement and other employee attitudes and behaviors are explained as components of an organizational system and their role in strategic nonprofit human resource management.

Coming up next, Chapter 2 offers a comprehensive review of the environment and the unique characteristics of nonprofit organizations and their employees. It explains why these contextual factors provide a natural setting for employee engagement. The chapter highlights the drivers of employee engagement, the link between employee engagement, and the management practices of nonprofit organizations. In Chapter 3, we present and explain a conceptual model for effective employee engagement in nonprofit organizations. The model draws on perspectives on employee engagement. The chapter briefly reviews employee engagement models and their relevance to nonprofit organizations. Chapter 4 explores how HR practices with emphasis on both the content and process can be deployed to facilitate employee engagement. The role of performance management, meaningfulness, and job enrichment in driving employee behavior and outcomes is explained in the chapter.

Chapter 5 examines the role, process, and challenges of engaging volunteers in nonprofit organizations. The chapter outlines the strategies for managing and engaging volunteers as part of the human resource pool of the organization. The chapter underlines the importance of volunteer engagement in fostering employee and stakeholder engagement. It highlights how employee engagement can be a tool for the recruitment and retention of volunteers. Chapter 6 explores the influence, role, and impact of board of directors of nonprofit organizations on employee engagement. We discuss how the board can help to support the employee engagement efforts of the organization, and work with management to develop employee engagement of board members. We will also highlight how the board can be a challenge in the employee engagement process and strategies to manage board employee engagement challenges. Chapter 7 focuses on the theories and practices of community engagement in nonprofit organizations. We highlight the characteristics and challenges of community engagement including the role of the environment that underlies nonprofit organizations. The chapter discusses how internal and external forces could shape the formation and deployment of community engagement to support the mission of the nonprofit organization.

Chapter 8 builds on the concepts and processes discussed in Chapter 4 to outline the tools nonprofit organizations can use to evaluate the outcomes and the impacts of employee engagement strategies. The chapter underlines the importance of multidimensional indicators of employee engagement and their relationship with nonprofit performance. Chapter 9 offer a relevant short employee engagement case to provide a compressive example of employee engagement drivers, implementation, and outcomes. The chapter complements the examples included in each chapter.

DISCUSSION QUESTIONS

1. What are the main perspectives that have been used to define employee engagement?
2. A nonprofit organization in your neighborhood has asked you to explain engagement as shared values to employees and volunteers. What are the features of shared values?
3. What are the benefits of employee engagement that you will emphasize to employees in your organization?
4. Why should an organization be concerned if they have many disengaged employees?

REFERENCES

Amah, E., & Ahiauzu, A. (2014). Shared values and organizational effectiveness: A study of the Nigerian banking industry. *Journal of Management Development, 33*(7), 694–708. https://doi.org/10.1108/JMD-09-2010-0065

Bailey, C., Madden, A., Alfes, K., & Fletcher, L. (2017). The meaning, antecedents and outcomes of employee engagement: A narrative synthesis. *International Journal of Management Reviews, 19*(1), 31–53.

Bakker, A. B. (2011). An evidence-based model of work engagement. *Current Directions in Psychological Science, 20*(4), 265–269. https://doi.org/10.1177/0963721411414534

Bakker, A. B., & Bal, M. P. (2010). Weekly work employee engagement and performance: A study among starting teachers. *Journal of Occupational and Organizational Psychology, 83*(1), 189–206. https://doi.org/10.1348/096317909X402596

Bakker, A. B., & Demerouti, E. (2007). The job demands-resources model: State of the art. *Journal of Managerial Psychology, 22*(3), 309–328. https://doi.org/10.1108/02683940710733115

Bakker, A. B., & Demerouti, E. (2008). Towards a model of work engagement. *Career Development International, 13*(3), 209–223. https://doi.org/10.1108/13620430810870476

Bakker, A. B., & Schaufeli, W. B. (2008). Positive organizational behavior: Engaged employees in flourishing organizations. *Journal of Organizational Behavior, 29*, 147–154.

Bakker, A. B., Van Emmerik, H., & Euwema, M. C. (2006). Crossover of burnout and engagement inwork teams. *Work and Occupations, 33*(4), 464–489.

Bakker, A. B., Hakanen, J. J., Demerouti, E., & Xanthopoulou, D. (2007). Job resources boost work engagement, particularly when job demands are high. *Journal of Educational Psychology, 99*(2), 274–284.

Baltzley, D. (2016). Purpose and shared values are the heart of employee engagement. *The Journal for Quality and Participation, 39*(3), 29–32.

Barrick, M. R., Thurgood, G. R., Smith, T. A., & Courtright, S. H. (2015). Collective organizational employee engagement: Linking motivational antecedents, strategic implementation, and firm performance. *Academy of Management Journal, 58*(1), 111–135.

Caldwell, M. (2012). Employee engagement and the transformation of the health care industry. In D. Shore (Ed.), *Forces of change: New strategies for the evolving healthcare marketplace*. Jossey-Bass.

Cartwright, S., & Holmes, N. (2006). The meaning of work: The challenge of regaining employee engagement and reducing cynicism. *Human Resource Management Review, 16*(2), 199–208. https://doi.org/10.1016/j.hrmr.2006.03.012

Costa, P., Passos, A. M., & Bakker, A. (2014). Empirical validation of the team work employee engagement construct. *Journal of Personnel Psychology, 13*, 34–45. https://doi.org/10.1027/1866-5888/a000102

Crawford, E. R., Lepine, J. A., & Rich, B. L. (2010). Linking job demands and resources to employee engagement and burnout: A theoretical extension and meta-analytic test. *Journal of Applied Psychology, 95*, 834–848.

Demerouti, E., Bakker, A. B., Nachreiner, F., Schaufeli, W. B. (2001, June). The job demands-resources model of burnout. *Journal of Applied Psychology, 86*(3), 499–512. PMID: 11419809.

Fredrickson, B. L. (2001, March). The role of positive emotions in positive psychology. The broaden-and-build theory of positive emotions. *American Psychologist, 56*(3), 218–226. https://doi.org/10.1037//0003-066x.56.3.218

Gibbons, J. (2006, November). *Employee engagement: A review of current research and its implications*. The Conference Board, Inc., 1–18. Retrieved on March 1, 2014.

Gorgievski, M. J., & Hobfoll, S. E. (2008). Work can burn us out or fire us up: Conservation of resources in burnout and employee engagement. In J. R. B. Halbesleben (Ed.), *Handbook of stress and burnout in health care* (pp. 7–22). Hauppauge.

Harter, J. K., Schmidt, F. L., & Hayes, T. L. (2002). Business-unit-level relationship between employee satisfaction, employee engagement, and business outcomes: A meta-analysis. *Journal of Applied Psychology, 87*(2), 268–279. https://doi.org/10.1037/0021-9010.87.2.268

Hatfield, E., Cacioppo, J., & Rapson, R. L. (1994). *Emotional contagion*. Cambridge University Press.

Hellriegel, D., & Slocum, J. W., Jr. (1974). Organizational climate: Measures, research and contingencies. *Academy of Management Journal, 17*(2), 255–280.

Hicks, R. (2011). *Recognizing the value of employee engagement* (Information Bulletin #152). Western Centre for Economic Research University of Alberta. ISBN 9781551958163.

House, R. J. (1997). Path-goal theory of leadership: Lessons, legacy, and a reformulated theory. *Leadership Quarterly, 7*, 323–352.

Kahn, W. A. (1990). Psychological conditions of personal employee engagement and disemployee engagement at work. *Academy of Management Journal, 33*, 692–724.

Kahn, W. A. (1992). To be fully there: Psychological presence at work. *Human Relations, 45*, 321–349.

Klein, H. J., Molloy, J. C., & Brinsfeld, C. T. (2012). Reconceptualizing workplace commitment to redress a stretched construct: Revisiting assumptions and removing confounds. *Academy of Management Review, 37*, 130–151.

Lages, C. R., Piercy, N. F., Malhotra, N., & Simões, C. (2020). Understanding the mechanisms of the relationship between shared values and service delivery performance of frontline employees. *The International Journal of Human Resource Management, 31*(21), 2737–2760. ISSN 1466-4399. https://doi.org/10.1080/09585192.2018.1464491.z. https://centaur.reading.ac.uk/75852/

Leiter, M. P., & Bakker, A. B. (2010). Work employee engagement: Introduction. In A. B. Bakker & M. P. Leiter (Eds.), *Work employee engagement: A handbook of essential theory and research* (pp. 1–9). Psychology Press.

LePine, J., Erez, A., & Johnson, D. (2002). The nature and dimensionality of organizational citizenship behavior: A critical review and meta-analysis. *Journal of Applied Psychology, 87*, 52–65.

Luthans, F., & Peterson, S. J. (2002). Employee engagement and manager self-efficacy: Implications for managerial effectiveness and development. *Journal of Management Development, 21*, 376–387. https://doi.org/10.1108/02621710210426864

Macey, W., & Schneider, B. (2008). The meaning of employee engagement. *Industrial & Organizational Psychology, 1*, 3–30.

Marks, M. A., Mathieu, J. A., & Zaccaro, S. J. (2001). A temporally based framework and taxonomy of team process. *Academy of Management Review, 26*, 356–376.

Maslach, C., & Leiter, M. P. (2008). Early predictors of job burnout and engagement. *Journal of Applied Psychology, 93*(3), 498–512. https://doi.org/10.1037/0021-9010.93.3.498

Maslach, C., Jackson, S. E., & Leiter, M. P. (1996). *Maslach burnout inventory manual*. Consulting Psychologists Press.

May, D. R., Gilson, R. L., & Harter, L. M. (2004). The psychological conditions of meaningfulness, safety and availability and the engagement of the human spirit at work. *Journal of Occupational and Organizational Psychology, 77*(1), 11–37.

McDonald, P., & Gandz, J. (1992). Getting value from shared values. *Organizational Dynamics, 20*(3), 64–77. ISSN 0090-2616. https://doi.org/10.1016/0090-2616(92)90025-I. https://www.sciencedirect.com/science/article/pii/009026169290025I

Michaelson, C., Pratt, M. G., Grant, A. M., & Dunn, C. P. (2014). Meaningful work: Connecting business ethics and organization studies. *Journal of Business Ethics, 121*(April 2013), 77–90. https://doi.org/10.1007/s10551-013-1675-5

Mowday, R. T., Porter, L. W., & Steers, R. M. (1982). *Employee-organization linkages: The psychology of commitment, absenteeism and turnover*. Academic Press.

Newton, P. (2015). *Employee engagement in Saskatchewan school divisions*. Imprint Saskatchewan Educational Leadership Unit, Department of Educational Administration, College of Education, University of Saskatchewan. Retrieved on December 2021, from https://saskschoolboards.ca/wp-content/uploads/Employee-engagement-Review-Report-2015.pdf

Niven, K. (2013). Affect. In M. D. Gellman & J. R. Turner (Eds.), *Encyclopedia of behavioral medicine*. Springer. https://doi.org/10.1007/978-1-4419-1005-9_1088

Okafor, C. (2008). Shared values and organizational performance of Nigerian companies: An empirical analysis. *Asian Journal of Scientific Research, 1*(3), 265–273.

Parker, P. D., & Martin, A. J. (2009). Coping and buoyancy in the workplace: Understanding their effects on teachers' work-related well-being and employee engagement. *Teaching and Teacher Education, 25*(1), 68–75. https://doi.org/10.1016/j.tate.2008.06.009

Piccolo, R. F., & Colquitt, J. A. (2006). Transformational leadership and job behaviors: The mediating role of core job characteristics. *Academy of Management Journal, 49*, 327–340.

Pitt-Catsouphes, M., & Matz-Costa, C. (2008). The multi-generational workforce: Workplace flexibility and employee engagement. *Community, Work and Family, 11*(2), 215–229. https://doi.org/10.1080/13668800802021906

Podolny, J. M., Khurana, R., & Hill-Popper, M. (2005). Revisiting the meaning of leadership. In B. M. Staw & R. Kramer (Eds.), *Research in organizational behavior* (Vol. 26, pp. 1–36). Elsevier Science.

Pratt, M. G., & Ashforth, B. E. (2003). Fostering meaningfulness in working and at work. In K. Cameron, J. E. Dutton, & R. E. Quinn (Eds.), *Positive organizational scholarship: Foundations of a new discipline* (pp. 308–327). Berrett-Koehler.

Rich, B. L., LePine, J. A., & Crawford, E. R. (2010). Job employee engagement: Antecedents and effects on job performance. *Academy of Management Journal, 53*, 617–635.

Reissner, S., & Pagan, V. (2013). Generating employee engagement in a public–private partnership: Management communication activities and employee experiences. *The International Journal of Human Resource Management, 24*(14), 2741–2759.

Robinson, D., Perryman, S., & Hayday, S. (2004). *The drivers of employee engagement*. Institute for Employment Studies.

Saks, A. M. (2006). Antecedents and consequences of employee engagement. *Journal of Managerial Psychology, 21*, 600–619.

Salamon, L., & Anheier, H. (1998). Social origins of civil society: Explaining the nonprofit sector cross nationally. *VOLUNTAS: International Journal of Voluntary and Nonprofit Organizations, 3*, 213–248.

Salanova, M., Agut, S., & Peiro, J. M. (2005). Linking organizational resources and work employee engagement to employee performance and customer loyalty: The mediation of service climate. *Journal of Applied Psychology, 90*, 1217–1227.

Schaufeli, W. B., & Bakker, A. B. (2004). *UWES–Utrecht Work Employee engagement Scale: Test manual* (Unpublished manuscript). Department of Psychology, Utrecht University, Utrecht, The Netherlands.

Schaufeli, W. B., Bakker, A., & Salanova, M. (2006). The measurement of work employee engagement with a short questionnaire: A cross-national study. *Educational and Psychological Measurement, 66*(4), 701–716.

Schaufeli, W. B., Salanova, M., Gonzalez-Roma, V., & Bakker, A. B. (2002). The measurement of employee engagement and burnout: A two sample confirmatory factor analytic approach. *Journal of Happiness Studies, 3*, 71–92.

Schmidt, F. (2009). *Employee engagement: A review of the literature*. Unpublished report prepared for the Office of the Chief Human Resources Officer, Treasury Board of Canada Secretariat.

Shuck, M. B. (2011). Four emerging perspectives of employee engagement: An integrative literature review. *Human Resource Development Review, 10*(3), 304–328.

Shuck, M. B., Reio, T. G., Jr., & Rocco, T. S. (2011). Employee engagement: An examination of antecedent and outcome variables. *Human Resource Development International, 14*, 427–445.

Shuck, M. B., & Wollard, K. (2010). Employee engagement & HRD: A seminal review of the foundations. *Human Resource Development Review, 9*, 89–110.

Steel, R. P., & Ovalle, N. K. (1984). A review of the meta-analysis of research on the relationship between behavioral intentions and employee turnover. *Journal of Applied Psychology, 69,* 673–686.

Swanberg, J. E., McKechnie, S. P., Ojha, M. U., & James, J. B. (2011). Schedule control, supervisor support and work engagement: A winning combination for workers in hourly jobs? *Journal of Vocational Behavior, 79*(3), 613– 624.

Towers Perrin. (2003a). *Winning strategies for a global workforce, attracting, retaining and engaging employees for competitive advantage.* Towers Perrin Global Workforce Study.

Towers Perrin. (2003b). *The 2003 Towers Perrin talent report: U.S. report. Understanding what drives employee engagement.* Stamford, CT.

Towers Watson. (2014, August). *The 2014 global workforce study driving employee engagement through a consumer-like experience.* Retrieved on February 2015, from https://www.towerswatson.com/en-CA/Insights/IC-Types/Survey-Research-Results/2014/08/the-2014-global-workforce-study

Truss, C., Shantz, A., Soane, E., Alfes, K., & Delbridge, R. (2013). Employee engagement, organisational performance and individual well-being: Exploring the evidence, developing the theory. *International Journal of Human Resource Management, 24*(14), 2657–2669.

Truss, C., Alfes, K., Delbridge, R., Shantz, A., & Soane, E. (Eds.). (2014). *Employee engagement in theory and practice.* Routledge.

Vakola, M., & Nikolaou, I. (2005). Attitudes towards organizational change: What is the role of employees' stress and commitment? *Employee Relations, 27*(2), 160–174. https://doi.org/10.1108/01425450510572685

Watrous, K. M., Huffman, A. H., & Pritchard, R. D. (2006). When coworkers and managers quit: The effects of turnover and shared values on performance. *Journal of Business and Psychology, 21*(1), 103–126.

Wu, T., & Wu, Y. J. (2019). Innovative work behaviors, employee engagement, and surface acting: A delineation of supervisor-employee emotional contagion effects. *Management Decision, 57*(11), 3200–3216.

Yalabik, Z. Y., Popaitoon, P., Chowne, J. A., & Rayton, B. A. (2013). Work employee engagement as a mediator between employee attitudes and outcomes. *International Journal of Human Resource Management, 24,* 2799–2823.

Zhang, X., & Bartol, K. M. (2010). Linking empowering leadership and employee creativity: The influence of psychological empowerment, intrinsic motivation, and creative process employee engagement. *Academy of Management Journal, 53*(1), 107–128.

CHAPTER 2

Nonprofit Organizations: The Land of Engagement

Nonprofit organizations are not only different entities in terms of their mission and values, they are also arguably different kinds of organizations in every way. For example, research suggests that nonprofits are organizations that are established by, organized around, and perform with significant interactions with a coalition of stakeholders. The effectiveness and competitive capabilities of nonprofit organizations depend to a significant extent on the strengths of the interactions with stakeholders, especially employees. Since employees and volunteers are the human capital of nonprofit organizations and a core factor in their social capital, the interactions that are required for the mission, the formulation and implementation strategy are inextricably linked to the degree of employee engagement. Therefore, for nonprofit organizations to be effective, to achieve their community problem-solving outcomes, and adapt to change in the fast-paced competitive environment, employee engagement is a core process in their human resources strategy and employment relations.

Nonprofit Organizations[1]

As organizations, nonprofits are a kaleidoscope. Nonprofits are diverse in scope, services, and in their interaction with the external environment. These factors suggest a certain level of complexity in the affairs of nonprofits. Thus, the discussion of employee engagement in nonprofit organizations needs to start with an understanding of the characteristics of nonprofit organizations, their employees, and volunteers. It is also critical to understand the workings of the systems and processes that facilitate the operations of nonprofits as well as the environment that shapes what they do and how they operate. Perhaps most relevant in the discussion of why engagement is a big deal for nonprofits is how employees navigate the unique environment of their organization.

Characteristics of Nonprofit Organizations

The characteristics of nonprofits point to the foundational pieces in the explanation of the context and processes of employee engagement in the sector. Therefore, the characteristics are relevant in the discussion of the full picture of why nonprofits must take engagement seriously.

Mission and Values
Nonprofit organizations are generally established for the primary purpose of achieving a *social mission*. The notion of social mission is simply another way of saying social purpose (Quarter, 1992). Although the nature and characteristics of what can be considered a social mission is endless to some extent, it is typically about meeting the social needs of people, doing good or simply providing social goods and services or access to the social goods and services (Salamon et al., 2000). Nonprofits are therefore established to address emergent problems and issues in society. The pertinent problems that nonprofit organizations aim to solve are generally those that the government and for-profit business organizations are either unable or unwilling to solve on their own or at all. Since the problems and issues in society are continuously evolving, nonprofit organizations must learn to adapt to change to facilitate their mission. So, while having a mission is important, the ability of a nonprofit to evolve, adapt, and align

---

[1] The sections on nonprofit organizations and nonprofit employees are adapted from Akingbola et al. (2019), Akingbola (2013a, 2013b).

the mission to the emergent problems in society is critical. How nonprofit organizations work to combine and manage resources, foster relationship with stakeholders and the community is fundamental to the mission. The social mission is the core of what people think about and emphasize when they talk about a nonprofit organization. Thus, the essence of a nonprofit organization lies in the mission. That is, the good cause the organization is set out to achieve. The example of Casa Familiar in Fig. 2.1 illustrates the unique values that underlie the mission and guide the services, policies, and practices of nonprofit organizations.

Nonprofit organizations are also about *values*. To facilitate the mission that constitutes the essence of the organization, nonprofits incorporate shared values that are derived from the shared norms and concerns in the community. The values that nonprofit organizations create through the translation of shared values are aimed at solving problems and changing the collective mindset (Smith & Lipsky, 1993) The values are the core principles and beliefs that guide and underlie the organizational activities and decision-making in nonprofit organizations. People, therefore, see nonprofit organizations as organizations that provide opportunities for individual such as employees, volunteers, and other stakeholders to actualize their values and commitments through participation in the activities

---

Example of Nonprofit Mission & Values

"We really operate like a family [with an attitude of] 'I got your back.' When we have to shift to meet needs, we do it by individuals stepping up and others supporting. This helps with the generational dynamics. We're community organizers first, perform in our positions second. Our core is in advocacy and community organizing, the highest priority above anything else."

Lisa Cuestas, Casa Familiar, San Ysidro, California

Sources:
Kanayama, K. (2020). Nonprofits, Transparency, and Staff Support in 2020: Three Case Studies. Nonprofit Quarterly. https://nonprofitquarterly.org/nonprofits-transparency-and-staff-support-in-2020-three-case-studies/

Fig. 2.1 Nonprofit mission and values

> **Adapting the mission**
>
> The Executive Director, Lisa Cuestas noted that " as the leading social service provider in a park-poor area, we got the support of donors and the PARC Foundation. The conversation can't be just about affordable housing; it's also about quality of life. The church is now a black box theater. Seniors, families, and couples live there. Baristas get training on site, and access to financial education and coaching" (Kanayama, 2020. p.2)
>
> Lisa Cuestas, Casa Familiar, San Ysidro,California
>
> Sources:
> Kanayama, K. (2020). Nonprofits, Transparency, and Staff Support in 2020: Three Case Studies. Nonprofit Quarterly. https://nonprofitquarterly.org/nonprofits-transparency-and-staff-support-in-2020-three-case-studies/

Fig. 2.2 Adapting the mission

of the organization (Jeavons, 1992). Typically, the values of the stakeholders and the nonprofit are aligned at the start of their interaction. However, a nonprofit can diversify and embrace new values that may not be consistent with the values of the employees, volunteers, and other stakeholders, over time (see Figs. 2.1, 2.2).

This suggests that the number one issue for the managers and employees of any nonprofit organization is how to ensure that the organization is positioned to achieve the mission. This means that doing the good the organization sets out to do is paramount. The mission and values are more than mere corporate statements. The mission is the basis of the systems, processes, and interactions that are central to the services and meeting the expectations of the stakeholders including employees and volunteers. Thus, the mission and values are essential to analyze, understand, and facilitate the ability of a nonprofit organization to adapt to change

Services and Roles

The mission of nonprofit organizations is translated into diverse social goods and services that are developed to meet the needs of the community. As noted above, the services that nonprofit organizations provide are often those, the government and for-profit business organizations are unable or unwilling to provide in areas such as social services, education, health, social justice, environment, and community economic development (Anheier, 2005). The specific services may include homeless services, mental health, disaster relief, youth, women and senior services. Nonprofit organizations are also the primary players in social enterprises. To illustrate the diverse scope of the services of nonprofits, Table 2.1 shows the mission and an overview of the services of three nonprofit organizations in the United States and Canada.

In addition to their services, nonprofit organizations are active in *political advocacy* especially for people who are marginalized and vulnerable such as seniors, children, visible minorities, LGBTQ, and people with disabilities. This role is particularly important because it emphasizes nonprofit organizations as change agents not only in terms of their mission but also their contribution to driving social change by advocating for public policy. While nonprofit organizations in different countries have variations in the degree of advocacy for the purpose of public policy, direct or indirect partnership with the government is an inherent characteristic of nonprofit organizations.

Nonprofit organizations are also the major players in the building of *social capital* in the community. This essentially describes how people build "social networks and the norms of reciprocity and trustworthiness that arise from them" (Putnam, 2000, p. 19). Social capital is enhanced by civic engagement or participation, and it is the basis of *community building*. Along the same line, nonprofit organizations are actively involved in connecting people to the political process which makes them an important player in the democratic process (Moulton & Eckerd, 2012). Altogether, the benefits of social capital and community building are a boon for society including for-profit business organizations.

The services and roles of nonprofit organizations emphasize their critical role in the social, *political,* and *economic* institutions in society. These general environment factors including *demography* and *culture* are industry factors for many nonprofit organizations because they directly affect the activities of the organization. Understanding the services and roles of nonprofit organizations and how they impact the core institutions of society is essential to understand change in the sector. The analysis of the process, content, and competencies of change must include the interrelated dimensions of the roles and services of nonprofit organizations.

Table 2.1 Services of nonprofit organizations

Organization	Mission	Services
Stone House, Roxbury, Massachusetts	Stone House makes a difference in our community by caring for and protecting adult and child survivors of domestic abuse, and helping them rebuild safe, secure, independent lives of purpose and self-fulfillment	– Crisis intervention – Advocacy and accompaniment – Sustained individual help – Financial stability – Immigration support – Support groups – Parenting/life skills education – Emergency shelter – Transitional housing – Permanent supportive housing – Rent-subsidized permanent housing – Housing search and placement – Stabilization – Rent subsidies – Family-strengthening activities – Case management and advocacy – Child care
Scarborough Centre for Healthy Communities, Scarborough, Ontario	SCHC is dedicated to meeting the diverse, holistic health needs of the communities of Scarborough by addressing the physical, mental, social, financial, and environmental aspects of their health. Through the promotion of healthy lifestyles and the delivery of a comprehensive range of culturally competent health and social services, we cultivate vital and connected communities	Community support services Health services Community initiatives
NeighborLink Indianapolis, Indiana	Our mission is simple, help senior homeowners in need and individuals with disabilities age in place safely and with dignity by providing home repairs at no cost to those homeowners	Homeless & Housing, Housing Support, Human Services, Senior Centers, Seniors

Environment of Nonprofit Organizations

General and competitive environment factors are relevant to understand the context of nonprofit organizations. General environment factors such as the economy, political, and sociocultural factors highlight how the broader environment trends are particularly important in nonprofit organizations. These factors are the underlying forces that coalesce with the industry indicators to shape organizational factors, job resources, and personal resources of employees. The nonprofit environment factors are relevant to understand the antecedents and consequences of employee engagement in nonprofit organizations. Below, we provide an overview of the general and industry environment factors and the internal forces in nonprofit organizations.

Community Needs

Community needs are continuously evolving. Driven by a variety of factors including demographic, social, and economic trends, community needs influence the mission and strategic direction of nonprofit organizations. The demographic factors such as age, level of education, income level, where people live, the family status of the people, and diversity define the type and level of community needs that influence the demand for the services of nonprofit organizations. Since nonprofit organizations are the products of the shared values and problem-solving needs of the society (Smith & Lipsky, 1993), what the community determines to be pertinent problems and the values they emphasize, shape the services of nonprofit organizations. Emergent community needs are a fundamental external environment factor for nonprofits. The services of nonprofits are established through emergent community needs with stakeholder engagement as a key part of the process. *New York Cares* exemplifies how a nonprofit organization must position itself to respond to emergent community needs. For example, *New York Cares* created a program called Community First with stakeholders to send resources and people directly to areas of New York City that has the most urgent needs (Fig. 2.3). They work with government agencies, activists, and residents, to listen, to understand the issues facing the neighborhoods, and deploy volunteers to make a meaningful, long-term difference in the communities of focus (Turkewitz, 2022).

The same trends that define community needs also underlie engagement in the internal environment of nonprofit organizations. For

> **New York Cares during Covid**
>
> In Brooklyn, the stress and trauma brought on by the pandemic has taken a toll on community members of all ages, especially children. Unfortunately, there are few resources to help people manage their mental health.
>
> Reading "helps children cope during times of stress and tragedy."
>
> In collaboration with United for Brownsville, New York Cares recently joined Brooklyn Book Bodega to distribute 5,000 books over three events, promoting literacy, education, and support for our young scholars. Our volunteers—many of whom were local to Brooklyn—hand-delivered 1,500 of those books.
>
> Adam Maldonado, New York Cares Community Engagement Associate
>
> Sources: Turkewitz, D. (2022). Communities First: Centering Service Where It's Needed Most. March 31, 2022 https://www.newyorkcares.org/blogs/communities-first-centering-service-where-it-s-needed-most

Fig. 2.3 New York cares adapt to community needs during COVID-19

example, demographic trends determine the pool of human resources available to nonprofit organizations for service delivery, management, and governance. Engagement plays an important role in how nonprofits attract, retain, and motivate their human resource pool.

Economy

The economy is a major factor for nonprofit organizations. What makes the economy to be unique in the nonprofit sector is that it can drive change at multiple dimensions of the organization including services and revenue. For example, COVID-19 brought significant economic impacts and necessitated many nonprofit organizations to implement strategies to adapt to the emerging challenges and shift in their operating environment (Imagine Canada, 2020). Due to the pandemic, many nonprofit organizations lost up to half of their revenue.

The economic downturn is also an environmental factor in terms of services (Foster & Meinhard, 2002). Ironically, the COVID-19 and downturn in the economy suggest that nonprofit organizations are more

2 NONPROFIT ORGANIZATIONS: THE LAND OF ENGAGEMENT   45

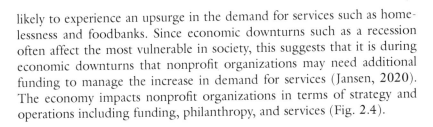

Fig. 2.4 COVID-19 and nonprofit revenue in Canada

likely to experience an upsurge in the demand for services such as homelessness and foodbanks. Since economic downturns such as a recession often affect the most vulnerable in society, this suggests that it is during economic downturns that nonprofit organizations may need additional funding to manage the increase in demand for services (Jansen, 2020). The economy impacts nonprofit organizations in terms of strategy and operations including funding, philanthropy, and services (Fig. 2.4).

Government Policy

For many nonprofit organizations, the government is the single most important stakeholder apart from the clients and the community. This close relationship between nonprofit organizations and government is a key factor in the mission, the type of services and the strategy that nonprofit organizations develop and implement. How the government interacts with nonprofit organizations is multifaceted and multilayered. It is often the case that the policy of the government in one domain will overlap with another policy area that is relevant to nonprofit organizations. To explain this many-sided role of government as an external factor in nonprofit organizations, we illustrate their impacts using three overlapping elements: funding; a measure of performance; and accountability.

Funding. Government funding is the largest source of revenue for many nonprofit organizations (Boris et al., 2010). The significant level of dependence on the government is a result of the public goods and services that nonprofit organizations provide. Moreover, research has consistently highlighted that the increased scope of the nonprofit sector is a by-product of the downloading of services that were previously provided by the government (Bennett & Savani, 2011). It is therefore not a surprise that the dependence on government funding is manifested in multiple elements of a nonprofit organization including services, strategy, and human resources management. A report by the Urban Institute found that 82% of nonprofit organizations in the study introduced change in response to a decrease in local, state, and federal government funding (Boris et al., 2010). However, government funding was important only in the survival of some nonprofits during COVID-19 (Faulk et al., 2021). The role of government funding as an external environment factor in nonprofits cannot be over-emphasized.

Performance standards. A standout in the way government funding affects nonprofit organizations is the measures of performance. Respective federal, state and local governments tend to move the goalpost of performance measures they attach to funding of nonprofit organizations in line with their values and agenda. They dictate the types of performance measures nonprofit organizations are required to use for reporting (Alexander et al., 2010). Often, the changes in performance measures are inconsistent with available empirical evidence and the standards currently used by nonprofit organizations. Nonprofit managers must implement practices on what and how they measure the performance of their services for the different levels of government. They must continuously adapt to new measures of performance depending on the agenda of the political party in power.

Accountability. Accountability is an upshot of the impact of government on the performance measures and outcomes of nonprofit organizations discussed above. To meet the requirements of government funding on reporting, nonprofit organizations develop and implement change in the administrative systems and processes of the organization. However, the scope of accountability that has evolved has engendered a shift in the culture of nonprofit organizations and the nature of the relationship with the government. Thus, accountability is another distinct way government is a major driver in nonprofit organizations. Although it has contributed to the awareness of quality management in nonprofit organizations, the real and lingering questions about the cost of accountability is a major challenge in change for most nonprofit organizations.

Funding, performance standards and accountability highlight how governments impact nonprofit organizations. The three dimensions of their interaction emphasize that government is an important environmental factor in nonprofit organizations. Government is also a factor in most of the other general and competitive environment factors that drive nonprofit organizations.

Competition
Irrespective of perspective and perception of the emerging dynamics of the sector, the operating environment of nonprofit organizations has become increasingly competitive (Castaneda et al., 2008; Chetkovich & Frumkin, 2003). Nonprofit organizations compete for government funding, foundation grants, donation from individuals and corporations, and even for the attention of the community. This means that nonprofit managers must pay particular attention to how the convergence of general environment factors such as the economy, government policies and sociocultural trends and industry factors create competition among nonprofit organizations. They must also understand the areas in which they compete with for-profit business organizations in addition to their nonprofit counterparts. Competition is therefore a critical driver for nonprofit organizations. It requires continuous alignment of services, internal systems, and processes in order to gain competitive advantage. It has been suggested that competition enhances the quality of governance in nonprofit organizations (Glaeser, 2003). Perhaps most important, competition drives the need for engagement in how the nonprofit deploys human capital to gain competitive advantage.

Technology
Almost no organization can escape the pace and widespread impact of technology today. However, the role of technology has been largely absent in the discourse about the efficiency and effectiveness of nonprofit organizations. A survey by *NetChange Consulting* on technology use by nonprofit organizations reported that "only 11% indicated that the way their organization manages digital is highly effective" (Mogus & Levihn-Coon, 2018). This lack of emphasis does not mean that nonprofit organizations can discount technology as a driver. On the contrary, the social mission of nonprofit organizations emphasizes the importance of communication between clients, employees, and volunteers to facilitate

service delivery. Since the way clients and other stakeholders communicate is changing due to technology, nonprofit organizations must adapt in order to connect with clients to create awareness, identify emergent needs, and engage the stakeholders to facilitate the mission. Moreover, nonprofit organizations must leverage technology to enhance the quality of internal communication with teams on the frontline and working groups that are established to develop plans to manage projects and processes.

The impact of technology on nonprofit organizations is therefore all-encompassing. This is evidenced by the emergence of a new term, a tech nonprofit. Tech nonprofit is described as an "emerging term that refers to a tech startup that is building software or web applications using a nonprofit model for social impact" (Udavant, 2022). Udavant illustrated nonprofits that are using technology to drive their mission and foster important social change (see Fig. 2.5). The need for nonprofit organizations to fully embrace digital technology to effectively deliver service, manage the collection, analysis and use of data cannot be overemphasized. From social media use in service delivery, fundraising, and advocacy to data analytics for decision-making in operations, human resources management, and strategy, technology is the harbinger of significant change in nonprofit organizations. It can help the organization to better adapt, manage, and innovate with digital trends (Fig. 2.6).

COVID-19 and Government Funding in the US

The average organization maintained its overall staff and total revenue in 2020, in part because of government support. But this was not the reality for all nonprofits, many of which experienced severe shocks to primary revenue streams and volunteer human resources. Forty percent of organizations reported losses in total revenue for 2020 (including 54 percent of arts organizations and 36 percent of all other nonprofits).

Sources: Faulk, L. et al., (2021). Nonprofit Trends and Impacts 2021. National Findings on Donation Trends from 2015 through 2020, Diversity and Representation, and First-Year Impacts of the COVID-19 Pandemic. Urban Institute

---

Fig. 2.5 COVID-19 and government funding

> **Technology and Nonprofit Organizations**
>
> Two other organizations making education more accessible to traditionally excluded populations are B*lack Sisters in STEM* (*Black SiS*) and *Empowr*. Both nonprofits are using tech to help students of color gain access to educational resources, readying them for high-paying careers.
>
> That's where the the *Asylum Seeker Advocacy Project* (*ASAP*) comes in. The nonprofit helps asylum seekers navigate the complex US immigration system by providing in-depth legal resources, breaking immigration news alerts, and a virtual legal help desk where members can ask immigration attorneys questions about their cases.
>
> Sources: Udavant, S. (2022). Why Tech Nonprofits Are Building Digital Tools for Racial Equity and Justice. Nonprofit Quarterly. August 2022. https://nonprofitquarterly.org/tech-nonprofits-building-digital-tools-racial-equity-racial-

Fig. 2.6 Technology and nonprofit organizations

Foundation of Nonprofit Employee Engagement
The overview of the characteristics and the factors in their external environment highlight the underlying factors of employee engagement in nonprofit organizations. The characteristics, the environment, and the industry factors together constitute the distinctive elements of the sector and explain nonprofits as inherently complex systems (Golden-Biddle et al., 2007). As complex systems, nonprofits are susceptible to the powerful forces of these multidimensional factors driven by a combination of their distinctive context, which requires them to deploy equally distinctive organizational and human resource management strategies and practices. This is basically the foundation of employee engagement in nonprofit organizations. Now that we have explained the foundational factors, the next section examines the main component of nonprofit employee engagement in terms of their centrality in the distinctive context of their organization. It is important to understand employees, *first*, as the core human resources of nonprofit organizations. *Second*, we also need to understand employees in terms of their characteristics and role in the context of nonprofit organizations, and *third*, we must also explain why

employees are the main subject of engagement as well as the most important player in the engagement that nonprofits must deploy to facilitate the mission and operations of the organization.

Nonprofit Core Human Resources[2]

People are at the core of the mission and values, services and roles, and the organizational processes of nonprofit organizations. The discussion of employee engagement is inextricably tied to the centrality of people in what nonprofits are about, how they run their operations and function as organizations. The employees and volunteers are the core human resources of nonprofit organizations (Akingbola, 2013b; Barbeito & Bowman, 1998; Light, 2003). The human resources comprising senior leadership, employees, and the board of directors, analyzes the external environment, determines the emergent needs or problems of the community, creates services based on the mission of the organization, create awareness among stakeholders, develop and implement the strategy of the organization. In addition, the pace of change in nonprofits in recent decades has amplified the centrality of people to help to position the organization to weather the threats and optimize the opportunities in the external environment. Hence, there has been a significant focus on the management of human resources (Akingbola, 2013a; Ridder & McCandless, 2010) and professionalization in nonprofits.

Importance of Employees and Volunteers
For the quintessential nonprofit, the core human resources of the organization are *volunteers, employees,* and *volunteer members* of the board of directors. Employees and volunteers are the human capital that the nonprofit deploys to identify the community needs to develop into services, to navigate funding relationships, to engage stakeholders and to guide the strategy that foster the mission. The volunteers provide governance for effective oversight of the management of nonprofit organizations. The employees and volunteers are arguably the most important players in understanding and managing the operations of nonprofit organizations. Nonprofit organizations cannot exist without the knowledge,

---

[2] The sections on nonprofit organizations and nonprofit employees are adapted from Akingbola et al. (2019), Akingbola (2013a, 2013b).

skills, and abilities as well as the commitment of the employees and volunteers. The competencies of the employees and volunteers will shape the core capabilities of a nonprofit and the continuous ability to align the mission to the changing needs of the community.

The importance of employees and volunteers suggest that nonprofits are a different context for employee engagement (Akingbola & van den Berg, 2019; Park et al., 2018). Moreover, different processes, types, and outcomes of engagement are likely to be at play due to the characteristics and context of nonprofits. Nonprofits are not only different entities in terms of their mission and values, but they are also arguably different kinds of organizations in every way. The effectiveness and competitive capabilities of nonprofit organizations depend to a significant extent on the strengths of the interactions with stakeholders especially employees. Since employees and volunteers are the human capital of nonprofit organizations and a core factor in their social capital, the interactions that are required for the mission, the formulation and implementation strategy are inextricably linked to the degree of employee engagement. Therefore, for nonprofit organizations to be effective, achieve their community problem-solving outcomes, strategic goals, and to facilitate change in the fast-paced competitive environment, employee engagement is key.

Characteristics of Nonprofit Employees

Beyond the centrality of their importance to the organization, nonprofit employees are different in several ways. From program planning, relationship with funders, service delivery, and program evaluation, the role and importance of employees and volunteers are multifaceted. In addition, nonprofit employees have behavioral characteristics that further reinforce their importance and critical role in the effectiveness of the organization (Akingbola, 2015). It also places employees at the top of the organizational resources available to nonprofits to deploy in their resource dependence relationship with the government and funders.

Mission Attachment

Employees are attracted and often choose to work for nonprofits because they identify with the mission and values of the organization (Brown & Yoshioka, 2003; McMullen & Schellenberg, 2003). The research further suggests that nonprofit employees tend to perceive their work as an opportunity to serve the public good and contribute to worthy causes.

From this perspective, nonprofits not only offer employment but also an opportunity for employees to actualize individual values. This inherent moral attachment plays an important role in the motivation of employees of nonprofits (Baluch, 2017; Light, 2002). Research suggests that nonprofit employees have a higher connection to the mission of the organization, public service motivation, and commitment than employees in business and public sector organizations (Light, 2002). Therefore, in nonprofits, the need to motivate employees who are committed to the mission of the organization is not as much a challenge as the need to sustain the level of motivation (Kim, 2005).

Intrinsic Motivation
One upshot of the inherent public service motivation, and the alignment of employee and organizational values is that extrinsic rewards are not the most important motivating factors for nonprofit employees (Parry et al., 2005; Roomkin & Weisbrod, 1999). Empirical research has found that compared to employees of for-profit organizations, employees of nonprofits are more likely to receive non-monetary rewards for their work (Borzaga & Tortia, 2006; Light, 2002; Schepers et al., 2005). Research also indicates that nonprofit employees place less emphasis on output-contingent incentives than for-profit organizations (Devaro & Brookshir, 2007). Hence, it has been suggested that nonprofit employees have a stronger non-monetary orientation (Devaro & Brookshir, 2007; Schepers et al., 2005). The intrinsic motivation and higher level of commitment, points to the role of social exchange in the relationship between employees and nonprofit organizations.

Donative Labor
Closely related to the intrinsic and public service motivation is the question of compensation in nonprofit organizations. Research indicates that wages are lower in nonprofits compared to for-profit organizations (Barbeito & Bowman, 1998; Jobome, 2006; McMullen & Schellenberg, 2003). It has been suggested that the difference in salary increases as the position moves from the clerical to the managerial level. At the managerial level, studies have found that wages are not only lower but are generally not related to performance (Ballou & Weisbrod, 2003; Devaro & Brookshir, 2007). One perspective explains the lower wages in nonprofits in terms of non-distribution constraint (Hansmann, 1980). According to this perspective, given that nonprofits do not distribute profit, senior

leadership and managers have limited discretion in terms of how they compensate and the level of compensation they offer employees (Mesch & Rooney, 2008). Non-distribution constraint also means that employees and managers are attracted to "an organization with goals other than profit maximization" (Roomkin & Weisbrod, 1999, p. 778). In essence, nonprofits benefit from the compensation effect of non-distribution constraints.

Therefore, it has been suggested that nonprofits adopt low wages to attract employees who are intrinsically motivated and committed to the goals of the organization (Handy & Katz, 1998). Nonprofits are also able to offer lower wages due to employees who are willing to donate their labor—donative labor hypothesis—for the mission of the organization (Hallock, 2002). Another explanation for the lower wages points to the public goods and services of nonprofits (Leete, 2001; Ruhm & Borkoski, 2003). From this perspective, it is the opportunity to provide public goods and services that is more important to employees than the wage rate of the organization. In other words, nonprofit employees emphasize social objectives and value orientation in terms of their compensation.

Employee Volunteer Partnership

It is not uncommon for nonprofits to commence operations with only volunteers and gradually integrate paid employees as they evolve in their organizational life cycle (Anheier et al., 2001). While the degree of partnership varies among nonprofits (Handy et al., 2008), the context is characterized by unique dynamics because of the partnership between employees and volunteers (Akingbola & Phaetthayanan, 2021). Research suggests that employees are not basically different from volunteers in terms of their work attitudes (Liao-Troth, 2001). They are likely to have similar job attitudes in terms of affective commitment, psychological contract, and organizational justice.

Beyond the work attitude, two main dimensions highlight distinctive characteristic of employee volunteer partnership. First, employees and volunteers interchange roles and responsibilities. Handy et al. (2008) found evidence that some tasks performed by employees and volunteers were interchangeable. Second, other research suggest that employees are replacing volunteers due to the increased professionalization of nonprofits in response to change in the funding environment (Akingbola & Phaetthayanan, 2021; Hall & Banting, 2000). The employee volunteer partnership portends a complex working relationship between employees and volunteers that may threaten employee morale (Akingbola & Phaetthayanan, 2021; Handy & Brudney, 2007). Often, the relationship with volunteers is a test of the organizational citizenship behavior of nonprofit employees.

Decision-Making

Nonprofits are built on the premise of collective action and participation. While there is debate on the extent to which these organizations are truly egalitarian and participatory in decision-making (Chaskin, 2003; Quarter et al., 2009), participatory structure and practices underlie the essential characteristic of nonprofits. The typical nonprofit offers the opportunity to participate in decision-making through teams and committees than for-profit organizations and embrace participation in decision-making to enhance employee buy-in (Kalleberg et al., 2006; Quarter et al., 2009). Hence employees expect nonprofits to embrace decision-making practices that support democratic culture (Brandel, 2001; Frumkin & Andre-Clerk, 2000).

In sum, nonprofit employees are distinctive in their motivation, commitment, and expectations. Their dispositional characteristics are reflected in their attitude toward compensation and are rooted in the social objectives and values that underlie the basic characteristics of nonprofit organizations. Understanding the dispositional characteristics of nonprofit employees is a fundamental contextual factor in the examination of nonprofit employee engagement.

Nonprofit General Engagement

An important part of the full picture of nonprofit employee engagement is the overall context of general engagement in these organizations. By general engagement, we mean the diverse processes of engagement that nonprofits use in their strategy, operations, and activities including in-service delivery, funding relationship, governance, and interactions with community stakeholders. This emphasizes that nonprofits have an inherent engagement orientation. The relevant discussion along this line relates to what are these engagement channels and what is the role of employees in these engagement processes. Below, we highlight examples of the general engagement orientation of nonprofits.

Nonprofit mission engagement. Irrespective of the type of public goods and services that the organization provides, the social mission is the core characteristic that is consistent in all nonprofit organization. Similarly, regardless of whether the mission of a nonprofit is intended to be an *expressive function* in which it serves the members or stakeholders in the organization or an *instrumental function* that is aimed at benefitting people regardless of whether they are members of the organization or not (Knutsen & Brower, 2010), nonprofit organizations are unique and dynamic entities that must engage stakeholders to survive. The organizational process of a nonprofit is embedded in the fundamental engagement that is necessitated by their mission. Nonprofits are characterized largely by the need to engage and collaborate. The nonprofit mission engagement is an imperative that nonprofits cannot avoid or discount.

Service delivery engagement. The service delivery process of nonprofit organizations emphasizes identifying the needs of clients with the inputs and active engagement of the clients. Hence, nonprofit services are not generally developed and delivered without the clients having some say in the process. Likewise, nonprofit organizations work closely with clients and stakeholders in their planning and strategic management process (Akingbola, 2006; McHatton et al., 2011). The emphasis on engagement and collaboration with clients ensures that the process of service delivery is consistent with the egalitarian values of nonprofit organizations.

Funding engagement. Funding is an inherently participatory process for many nonprofit organizations. Although mainstream nonprofit organizations generate less funding from individual philanthropy and corporations than from the government in many developed countries, the process of fundraising involves significant engagement of all players. Nonprofit organizations engage corporate and individual donors by keeping them abreast of relevant developments in the organization, especially in their services. In the funding relationship with the government and foundations, the interaction requires nonprofit organizations to engage the funder in the formal contractual working relationship. The ability of a nonprofit to build a collaborative partnership with the funding organization is important to overcome the challenges of funding. Also important are the roles of such collaborative relationships in the effort of the nonprofit to adapt to the continuous change in the funding environment.

Governance engagement. Perhaps, one process that most exemplifies the core ways nonprofit organizations are unique in addition to the mission and values is governance. In governance, decision-making typically involves stakeholders who have an important role in the decision that is being made such as employees, frontline volunteers, and clients. A good nonprofit board of directors must understand that nothing disengages stakeholders more than excluding those who are directly accountable and/or impacted by the decision. The levels of involvement in governance decision-making in a nonprofit could range from having a seat on the board to having a channel to offer suggestions. If the stakeholders are only informed about the issues or problems, and then asked to provide information that will help the decision-making, there is some level of involvement in the process.

Management engagement. Decision-making in nonprofit organizations is based on the premise of involvement and participatory feedback. The decision-making process on critical issues such as service delivery and funding the organization generally involves employees and the board of directors. These processes not only highlight involvement as an effective method of decision-making, but they are also consistent with the mission and values of nonprofit organizations helps to remove barriers in terms of leveraging the human and social capital of employees and volunteers to enhance the quality of decisions (Akingbola, 2013a). The need to understand engagement and effectively engage employees, requires the direct involvement of employees, volunteers, and other stakeholders. Figure 2.7 shows how a nonprofit is giving employees a voice to drive the mission of the organization.

Giving employees a voice

"We make sure our staff understand how we make decisions, have clarity on which ones staff control. Staff had a voice in how we set our COVID-19 prevention policy. It's an ongoing process, where we check in to see if it's working. We meet every day at nine a.m., offer multiple ways to raise issues, and will create more vehicles for our staff to have a say." (Kanayama, 2020. p.4)

Sheheryar Kaoosji, executive director of WWRC, Ontario, California

Sources:
Kanayama, K. (2020). Nonprofits, Transparency, and Staff Support in 2020. Three Case Studies. Nonprofit Quarterly. https://nonprofitquarterly.org/nonprofits-transparency-and-staff-support-in-2020-three-case-studies/

Fig. 2.7 Giving employees a voice

The general engagement orientation is the final stone in the foundational blocks of employee engagement in nonprofit organizations. It highlights the convergence of values-based orientation of involving stakeholders, with strategic, and operational needs to build relationships that will facilitate the mission of the organization. Now that the stage has been set, the next section explores the why, what, and how of employee engagement in nonprofit organizations. Employees are arguably the main subject of engagement as well as the most important player in the engagement that nonprofits must deploy to facilitate the mission and operations of the organization.

Nonprofits: Land of Employee Engagement

The combined effect of the characteristics, the environment, the contextual sector factors, and the centrality of people, particularly, employees and volunteers, highlight the multidimensional underlying factors of employee engagement in nonprofit organizations. Together with the general engagement orientation in these organizations, the combination of nonprofit characteristics, contextual factors, and the unique orientation of employees suggest that engagement is embedded within the complex social systems of nonprofits (Akingbola, 2013a). Therefore, employee engagement should be of critical importance in the strategy, policies, and practices of nonprofit organizations. The multidimensional factors of environment, organizational, and employee factors also suggest that employee engagement should permeate the culture of nonprofit organizations. To further explain the importance of employee engagement, we identify specific factors why employee engagement should be critical in the nonprofit organization by highlighting how the characteristics of nonprofits are embedded in the definitions of engagement discussed in Chapter 1.

Why Nonprofit Employee Engagement

First, nonprofits provide social goods and services. Thus, the business of nonprofits is labor intensive in nature. The implication is that nonprofits cannot substitute the human capital they require to provide their services with investment in physical capital (Akingbola, 2015). As a result, human capital often constitutes the core asset of the nonprofit organization (Akingbola, 2006; Light, 2003). This core characteristic of nonprofits highlights one angle of the importance of the link between individual employee's cognitive, emotional, and behavioral state and their work roles. In other words, nonprofits need engagement because the nature of their social mission requires employees to apply the personal self in their work roles.

Second, the mission of nonprofits is primarily aimed at achieving social objectives (Drucker, 1992; Quarter, 1992). In effect, the strategic goals that underlie the jobs and interactions of employees are therefore driven not only by organizational performance but also by the social causes and community needs that the nonprofit advocates to address. Nonprofits, therefore, expect employees not only to be engaged in their job roles but also in the community and with the stakeholders that shape the organization. The vigor, dedication, and absorption that (Schaufeli et al., 2002, p. 74) define as characteristics of employee engagement are important in both the job role, stakeholder interactions, and the advocacy role to support the organizational goals and the social mission of the nonprofit.

Third, for many small nonprofits, a comprehensive HRM system is out of the question. In these nonprofits, the organization is unable to provide any formal HRM support (Clark, 2007; McMullen & Schellenberg, 2002). HR practices are basically at an informal phase in which the quality of interpersonal relationships between employees and other stakeholders shapes the system (Akingbola, 2013b). Employee engagement provides a unique opportunity for the organization to connect with employees. It could facilitate engagement that is truly individually oriented which could enhance a strong internal fit for the HR system of the organization.

Fourth, there is also an inherent nexus between some of the elements of employee engagement and the egalitarian characteristic of nonprofits. Nonprofits are established on the premise of participation in decision-making (Kalleberg et al., 2006). Research has found that nonprofits generally tend to provide employees with the opportunity to participate in decision-making (Akingbola, 2013a; Kalleberg et al., 2006; Quarter et al., 2009). Thus, nonprofit employees expect to be involved in the decision-making of the organization. This expectation is translated into motivation and commitment to the organization.

The point of these specific factors is to illustrate how the central questions in engagement overlap with some of the key constructs that define the characteristics and context of nonprofits. It also provides insights into how the context of a nonprofit provides a natural setting for employee engagement. Employees of nonprofits expect to be engaged in their job and the organization. The role of multidimensional contextual factors is critical in the manifestation of nonprofit employee engagement.

Antecedents of Nonprofit Employee Engagement

Broadly, the characteristics and context of nonprofit organizations underlie the antecedents of employee engagement in the sector (Akingbola, 2017). Importantly, the multidimensional contextual factors are perhaps so critical in the manifestation of nonprofit employee engagement that some of the factors could be antecedents of collective organizational and team engagement. Nonetheless, the factors are intertwined with individual factors in the research on nonprofit engagement. A growing body of nonprofit research has identified specific antecedents of employee engagement in nonprofit organizations (Akingbola & van den Berg, 2019; Park et al., 2018; Selander, 2015). Building on our understanding of the basic characteristics of nonprofit organizations and the unique characteristics of nonprofit employees discussed in this chapter, we draw on research evidence to examine the antecedents of nonprofit employee engagement.

Mission Attachment
As discussed above, a key characteristic of nonprofit employees is their attachment to the mission of the organization (Brown & Yoshioka, 2003; Maulhardt et al., 2015). This attachment to the mission attracts employees and influences the decision of employees to work with the nonprofit organization. Since employees tend to perceive their work as an opportunity to serve the public good and contribute to worthy causes, the mission attachment provides motivation for the investment of their cognitive, behavioral, and emotional energy (Akingbola & van den Berg, 2019). The attachment to the mission could therefore play an important role in employee engagement.

Research has shown that employee mission attachment measured as public service motivation is related to employee engagement in nonprofit organizations (Selander, 2015; Svensson et al., 2021). Employees are energized to deploy discretionary effort to support the mission of the nonprofit organization. Moral attachment contributes to employee engagement to enhance the importance of their job role and facilitates higher connection to the mission of the organization. The relationship between public service motivation and engagement also means that employee commitment to the community needs that underlie the mission of the nonprofit organization is enhanced.

Value Congruence

Like mission, shared values are at the core of nonprofit organizations. The incorporation of a nonprofit organization is the actualization of translating shared values into actions that involve problem-solving activities in the community (Smith & Lipsky, 1993). It is those values that founders share that guide the efforts to establish an organization, what the organization is all about, and how it makes a difference. Thus, the values are a source of connection for the employees of the organization. Value congruence means the values of employees are aligned or fit the values of the nonprofit organization. It also means that employees share similar values with their coworkers. Therefore, value congruence is one of the means through which employees find meaning in their job, interactions with coworkers, and their relationship with the organization.

Since meaningfulness is one of the outcomes of the value congruence between employees and nonprofits, the organization is a platform for employees to actualize the values they share. Employees expect the organization's services, policies, and practices to be opportunities for them to live their personal altruistic values (Brown & Yoshioka, 2003; Newton & Mazur, 2016). Employees deem it worthy to invest their physical, cognitive, and emotional energy in the mission of the organization if they buy into the values of the nonprofit. In effect, the organization is the conduit for making a difference in society. If they identify with the values of the organization, employees are more likely to bring their whole self to their job and associate their self-image with the job and the organization. In other words, employees are likely to have higher level psychological availability and safety. Therefore, nonprofit employees who have value congruence with the organization are more likely to experience higher level of engagement. Another way of explaining this relationship between value congruence and engagement is that nonprofit shared values are organizational resources that contribute to the level of engagement of employees (Akingbola & van den Berg, 2019). Nonprofit value congruence is associated with performance (Helmig et al., 2015). The relationship with employee engagement could even mean a higher level of performance.

Job Characteristics and Demands

The fundamental characteristics of nonprofit jobs include components that shape not only what employees do, but also how they must adapt what they do in the context of nonprofits. The characteristics and demands could contribute to a higher level of engagement. First, nonprofit jobs are characterized by interpersonal transactions which are evidenced in the strategic and operational activities of the organization such as advocacy, funding, and interaction with clients (Akingbola, 2015). For example, when an employee provides support to a vulnerable client, the transaction often requires the use of emotional capital.

Second, jobs in nonprofits tend to require a mix of unique competencies to meet the requirements of complex organizational contexts in the sector (Akingbola, 2006; Herman, 2004). Nonprofit managers must focus not only on basic management functions such as budgeting, planning, decision-making, and supervision, but they and the employees of nonprofits must also learn to work with stakeholders including volunteer board of directors, advocacy groups, and multiple funding organizations (Akingbola, 2013a; O'Neill & Young, 1988). Moreover, nonprofit employees must learn to cope with the unpredictability of funding in their jobs and precarious employment relations derived from the changing institutional and regulatory demands (Cunningham, 2016). The unique competencies required in nonprofit organizations are job demands that underlie the job requirements and influence the behavioral expectations from employees in their jobs.

Three, nonprofit employees have the perception that due to the mission and values of their organization, egalitarian and participatory in decision-making will be the norm on the job and in work activities (Chaskin, 2003; Quarter et al., 2009). Research has somewhat backed this expectation by suggesting that nonprofits are more likely to offer an opportunity for employees to participate in decision-making through teams and committees than for-profit organizations (Akingbola, 2013a; Kalleberg et al., 2006). What this inherent expectation does is to lay the foundation for the deployment of discretionary effort that characterizes employee engagement. When employees know that what is expected is what they are experiencing in a nonprofit organization, they are like to be motivated to their discretionary effort.

Together, the characteristics and job demands of nonprofits are potentially important factors in the level of engagement of the employees. Because nonprofit jobs involve challenging work that incorporates variety, allows for the use of different skills and personal discretion, and provides the opportunity to make important contributions, meaningfulness, safety, and availability may be induced (Kahn, 1990, 1992). Research has highlighted that job characteristics contribute to engaged nonprofit employees' experience of job satisfaction and demonstration of behaviors that are consistent with organizational commitment, and organizational citizenship behavior (Akingbola & van den Berg, 2019). Engaged nonprofit employees are less likely to have the intention to quit.

Conversely, research suggests that job demands in nonprofit organizations are negatively related to the level of engagement of employees (Selander, 2015). The job demands that are related to employment relations are a disincentive for employee engagement. However, the same research found that the insecurity that is common in nonprofit employment relations may not significantly affect the level of employee engagement. While the job characteristics of nonprofits are related to employee engagement, the job demands are potential barriers to engagement in nonprofit organizations.

Intrinsic Motivation

As discussed above, nonprofit employees derive motivation from the opportunity to participate in a social mission, contribute to public good, and live their values through the values of the organization (Devaro & Brookshire, 2007; Ridder & McCandless, 2010). Therefore, nonprofit employees tend to emphasize intrinsic motivation than monetary rewards and recognition for their efforts (Baluch, 2017; Word & Carpenter, 2013). This could explain the need for nonprofits to balance the extent to which they deploy intrinsic and extrinsic rewards in their compensation system (Akingbola, 2015). Unlike the economic exchange that characterizes extrinsic reward such as compensation and benefits (Aryee et al., 2002), nonprofit motivation requires intrinsic reward and recognition to align the motivation of nonprofit employees with the HR strategy of the organization (Akingbola, 2015; Pichault & Schoenaers, 2003).

Consequently, nonprofit employees expect factors that contribute to intrinsic motivation such as egalitarian policies and practices, a work environment that actualizes their values, and the opportunity to contribute to social causes, to be emphasized by the organization (Quarter et al., 2009; Schepers et al., 2005). This is the root of social exchange in nonprofit organizations. If employees develop a reciprocal obligation based on their perception that the organization is meeting their social purpose expectation, coupled with their orientation for intrinsic reward, this could facilitate a sense of return on investment for their physical, cognitive, and emotional energy (Saks, 2006). Considering that individual employees have varied perceptions of the benefits they receive from their job and the organization, engagement is related to the extent to which nonprofit employees perceive a greater opportunity for intrinsic motivation (Akingbola & van den Berg, 2019; Svensson et al., 2021). The research suggests that the expectation of nonprofit employees in terms of intrinsic motivation contribute to their perception of social exchange that is more than the traditional exchange that is focused on trust, fairness, and respect in policies. Nonprofit employees expect actual social impact and progressive organizational practices.

The antecedents of nonprofit employee engagement are high-level factors that underlie the experience of engagement. Employees deploy their physical, emotional, and cognitive energy due to the attachment they have to the mission and values of nonprofit organizations. Also, the evidence that nonprofit employees draw on their intrinsic motivation and expectation of social exchange to determine their level of engagement highlight the process that is relevant in the context of nonprofits. The antecedents reinforce the understanding of how contextual factors can translate into, the level of nonprofit employee engagement.

Benefits of Nonprofit Employee Engagement

The benefits of nonprofit employee engagement generally consist of what employees and the organization gain because of engagement. Like for-profit businesses and public sector organizations, nonprofit organizations derive benefits from the level of engagement of their employees. The consequences of engagement also benefit the employees in many ways at the individual and collective team levels. Each of the benefits of employee engagement overlaps with the others and has multiplier effects on the services, policies, and practices of the organization. Following the list of benefits of employee engagement discussed in Chapter 1, we draw on research to highlight the specific benefits of employee engagement in nonprofit organizations. The benefits provide insight from research into why employee engagement is important in strategic human resource management and employment relations in nonprofit organizations.

Nonprofit Engagement: What is in it for employees?
Nonprofit employees stand to gain from their experience and level of engagement in the organization. The combination of the basic characteristics of nonprofits, the characteristics of employees, and the importance of their role in the organization suggest that engagement will have a stronger impact on employees. In effect, irrespective of the antecedents, employees of nonprofits will benefit from engagement. We explain the benefits that have been highlighted in research.

Job satisfaction. Due to their unique characteristics including attachment to the mission and values of the organization, the job satisfaction of nonprofit employees is directly related to their level of engagement. Therefore, research has shown that nonprofit employees experience job satisfaction when they are engaged (Akingbola & van den Berg, 2019). For nonprofit employees, job satisfaction results from the cognitive, emotional, and affective energy that they deploy in their job and the interactions in the organization. The characteristics and dimensions of the job facilitate reciprocity and interdependence in the process of job satisfaction (Rich et al., 2010). Employee perception of the mission, values, and context of the nonprofit contribute to their job satisfaction (Borzaga & Tortia, 2006; Melnik et al., 2013). Engagement means employees think positively and feel good about their job and their organization.

Well-being. Well-being is one of the outcomes of engagement that directly benefits the employee. Nonprofit employees have raised concerns about the disconnect between the espoused values and practices of their organization. This contributes to job dissatisfaction, and stress, and affects the well-being of the employees. (Baluch, 2017; Howe & McDonald, 2001; Kim, 2005). Therefore, employee engagement is particularly important to alleviate the concerns about employee psychological well-being in nonprofits. Research evidence has highlighted the role of engagement in employee well-being. When employees are engaged, they are more likely to report a higher level of psychological well-being (Svensson et al., 2021). Engagement enhances employees' positive perception of the job and the organization which contributes to how they manage the stress of the job role and the organization. Thus, engagement benefits employee well-being. The organization also benefits directly from the impact of engagement on the well-being of employees in terms of lower absenteeism.

Meaningfulness. Perhaps the most important benefit of engagement for nonprofit employees is meaningfulness. Meaningfulness underlies employees' public service motivation and their attachment to the mission of the nonprofit. It is why employees are working in the nonprofit organization and a key component of what they expect to get in return for their labor (Borzaga & Tortia, 2006; McDermott et al., 2013). Therefore, engagement is beneficial to nonprofit employee engagement because it is related and influenced significantly by the meaningfulness they experience in their job and the opportunity to actualize the mission and the values of the organization. The perception of the value, relevance, and importance of the job and the organization induces the investment of physical, cognitive, and emotional energy (Akingbola & van den Berg, 2019). This exemplifies the importance of social exchange in nonprofit organizations.

Employees are quite aware of the benefits that they and their organization derive from engagement. Individual employees are cognizant of and want to be engaged to enhance the quality of their work life. Like employees in other sectors, nonprofit employees know that engagement could help to mitigate burnout, facilitate positive emotions, and behaviors as well as enhance the perception of their team and the organization.

Nonprofit Engagement: What is in it for organizations?
Similar to employees, the benefits of employee engagement discussed in Chapter 1 are relevant in nonprofit organizations. Nonprofit organizations benefit from the enhanced productivity, improved customer satisfaction, the decreased rate of workplace accidents, and other relevant outcomes that engagement could facilitate. Beyond these, research has noted some specific outcomes of employee engagement for nonprofit organizations.

Organizational commitment. There are three forms of commitment: affective, continuance, and normative (Meyer & Allen, 1991). These three forms of commitment broadly explain the different ways employees are committed to the organization. Research has found that the three forms of commitment are related to employee and organizational outcomes (Meyer et al., 2002). However, except for the negative relationship of the three types of commitment with turnover and withdrawal cognition, research suggests that affective commitment has a positive relationship with the employee and organizational outcomes. The meaningful and family-like connection that employees develop with the organization could facilitate relevant outcomes for the job, the employee, and the organization (Macey & Schneider, 2008). Research has specifically indicated that commitment is an outcome that is mediated by job and organization engagement in a nonprofit organization (Akingbola & van den Berg, 2019). Engagement fosters an add-on to the inherent commitment that employees have to the nonprofit organization based on the mission and values (Light, 2002). Nonprofit employee engagement therefore further facilitates a pool of human resources that is committed to the organization. The value-added benefits of engagement to a nonprofit organization are more affective, continuance, and normative commitment.

Organizational citizenship behavior (OCB). OCB is characterized by behaviors such as helpfulness, sportsmanship, conscientiousness, and civic virtue (Organ, 1988). These behaviors facilitate an enabling environment and contribute to job and organizational performance (LePine et al., 2002; Macey & Schneider, 2008). Research has shown that employee engagement is related to OCB in nonprofit organizations (Akingbola & van den Berg, 2019; Park et al., 2018). Nonprofit employee engagement fosters OCB through the inherent social exchange between the organization and the employees. Again, nonprofit organizations benefit from engagement because, engaged employees tend to exhibit voluntary behavior such as helpfulness, conscientiousness, and civic virtue. These behaviors are derived from the attachment of the employees to the mission of nonprofit organizations which suggests that engagement is a benefit that enhances the connection of the employee to the nonprofit organization.

Intention to quit. Intention to quit is a strong indicator of an employee's future behavior (Carmeli & Weisberg, 2006). Therefore, it is an antecedent of voluntary turnover. Research has indicated that intention to quit is the best predictor of actual turnover, more so than satisfaction or commitment (Steel & Ovalle, 1984). In nonprofit organizations, contextual factors that are specific to the sector contribute to the intention to quit and turnover (Selden & Sowa, 2015). As discussed above employee well-being, the disconnect between the espoused values, and practices of nonprofit organizations contributes to job dissatisfaction, and stress, and affects the well-being of employees. (Baluch, 2017; Howe & McDonald, 2001; Kim, 2005). The same factors play an important role in the intention of nonprofit employees to quit the organization. However, research has found that employee engagement has a positive impact on intention to quit in nonprofit organizations (Akingbola & van den Berg,

2019; Park et al., 2018; Svensson et al., 2021). Nonprofit employees who are engaged are less likely to indicate an intention to quit. The research further emphasizes that irrespective of antecedents, engagement has a direct impact on intention to quit in nonprofit organizations (Akingbola & van den Berg, 2019). Therefore, engagement contributes to lower levels of employee turnover in nonprofit organizations. It contributes to employee retention with all the added advantages for the human resource management outcomes of the organization.

Innovative Work Behavior. Nonprofit organizations are inherently innovative organizations. Nonprofits develop innovative services, community-led initiative, funding activities, and alternative ways of organizing (Moore & McKee, 2012; Moore & Mullins, 2013). Regardless of the types of nonprofits, they have varying levels of innovation that may be related to the influence of the environment such as changing community needs, relationships with the government, and funders. Innovation could also be driven by other environmental and organizational factors. Regardless of the factors that necessitated it, there is increased emphasis on innovation in nonprofits and the innovation impacts client outcomes and the mission of the organization (McDonald, 2007; Shier & Handy, 2015). Employees are at the forefront of innovation in nonprofit organizations. Employees deploy their cognitive, emotional, and behavioral energy to find innovative solutions to emergent community needs, problems, issues, and processes (Saks, 2006; Shuck et al., 2014). However, the ability of nonprofit employees to deploy innovative behavior is dependent on the state of motivation of the employees and their leader's ability to foster an enabling internal environment for innovation (Berzin et al., 2016; Shier et al., 2018). Engagement facilitates innovative behavior of nonprofit employees which benefits the organization and the community. The need for innovative work behavior of employees is particularly heightened in the highly precarious operating environment of nonprofit organizations.

Conclusion

Nonprofit organizations are distinctive in their mission, services, and the multidimensional nature of their environment. In addition, nonprofit employees are also distinct in their mindset especially in their motivation to work for the organization and on the job in the organization. The relationship between these factors highlights the complexity of nonprofit organizations and the foundational elements of employee engagement. The chapter explains why the factors are particularly relevant to understand employee engagement in nonprofit organizations. After the discussion of the foundational elements of engagement, the chapter examines nonprofit employees in terms of their centrality in the distinctive context of their organization and outlines the general forms of engagement that nonprofits use in the operations of the organization. The chapter notes that general engagement highlights why nonprofits have an inherent engagement orientation. The specific factors why employee engagement should be critical in nonprofit organizations explain how the characteristics of nonprofits are embedded in the definitions of engagement discussed in Chapter 1. The specific antecedents of nonprofit employee engagement such as mission attachment and intrinsic motivation mirror the distinct contextual factors that underlie what nonprofit organizations are about. In the same vein, the benefits of employee engagement enhance our understanding of the dimensions of engagement for employees, managers, and stakeholders of nonprofit organizations.

Discussion Questions

1. What are the unique characteristics of nonprofit organizations?
2. How would you explain factors that differentiate nonprofit employees from employees in other sectors?
3. What are the benefits of employee engagement that you think nonprofit employees will find valuable?
4. Explain one antecedent of employee engagement that is unique to nonprofit organizations or nonprofit employees?
5. Do you think nonprofit employees need more or less engagement?

References

Akingbola, K. (2006). Strategy and human resource management in nonprofit organizations: Evidence from Canada International. *International Journal of Human Resource Management, 17*(10), 1707.

Akingbola, K. (2013a). A model of strategic nonprofit human resource management. *Voluntas: International Journal of Voluntary and Nonprofit Organizations, 24*, 214–240.

Akingbola, K. (2013b). Contingency, fit and flexibility of HRM in nonprofit organizations. *Employee Relations, 35*(5), 479–494.

Akingbola, K. (2015). *Managing human resources for nonprofits.* Routledge.

Akingbola, K. (2017). Employee engagement and job satisfaction. In J. Sowa & J. Word (Eds.), *The nonprofit human resource management handbook: From theory to practice.* Routledge.

Akingbola, K., & Phaetthayanan, S. (2021). The paradox of employee–volunteer interchangeability in a supported social enterprise. *Journal of Public and Nonprofit Affairs, 17*(1), 89–107. https://doi.org/10.20899/jpna.x.x.xxx-xxx

Akingbola, K., & Van Den Berg, H. A. (2019). Antecedents, consequences, and context of employee engagement in nonprofit organizations. *Review of Public Personnel Administration, 39*(1), 46–74. https://doi.org/10.1177/0734371X16684910

Akingbola, K., Rogers, S., & Baluch, A. (2019). *Change management in nonprofit organizations: Theory and practice.* Palgrave Macmillan.

Alexander, J., Brudney, J., & Yang, K. (2010). Introduction to the symposium: Accountability and performance measurement: The evolving role of nonprofits in the hollow state. *Nonprofit Management and Leadership, 39*(4), 565–570.

Anheier, H. (2005). *Nonprofit organizations theory management policy.* Routledge.

Anheier, et al. (2001). The new geography of global civil society: NGOs in the world city network. *Journal of International Globalization, 1,* 265–277.

Aryee, S., Budhwar, P. S., & Chen, Z. X. (2002). Trust as a mediator of the relationship between organizational justice and work outcomes: Test of a social exchange model. *Journal of Organizational Behavior, 23*(3), 267–85.

Ballou, J. P., & B. A. Weisbord. (2003). Managerial rewards and behavior of for-profit, governmental and nonprofit organizations: Evidence from the hospital industry. *Journal of Public Economics, 87,* 1895–1920.

Baluch, A. M. (2017). Employee perceptions of HRM and well-being in nonprofit organizations: Unpacking the unintended. *The International Journal of Human Resource Management, 28,* 1912–1937.

Barbeito, C. L., & Bowman, J. P. (1998). *Nonprofit compensation and benefits practices.* John Wiley.

Bennett, R., & S. Savani. (2011). Surviving mission drift: How charities can turn dependence on government contract funding to their own advantage. *Nonprofit Management and Leadership, 22*(2), 217–231.

Berzin, S., Pitt-Catsouphes, M., & Gaitan-Rossi, P. (2016). Innovation and sustainability: An exploratory study of intrapreneurship among human service organizations. *Human Service Organizations: Management, Leadership & Governance, 40,* 540–552.

Boris, E. T., de Leon, E., Roeger, K. L., & Nikolova. M. (2010). *Human service nonprofits and government collaboration: Findings from the 2010 national survey of nonprofit government contracting and grants*. The Urban Institute. Retrieved from December 2013, http://www.urban.org/uploadedpdf/412 228-nonprofit-governmentcontracting.pdf.

Borzaga, C., & Tortia, E. (2006). Worker motivation, job satisfaction and loyalty in public and nonprofit social services. *Nonprofit and Voluntary Sector Quarterly, 35,* 225–248.

Brandel, G. A. (2001). The truth about working in not-for-profit. *CPA Journal, 71*(10), 13.

Brown, W. A., & Yoshioka, C. (2003). Mission attachment and satisfaction as factors in employee retention. *Nonprofit Leadership and Management, 14*(1), 5–18.

Carmeli, A., & Weisberg, J. (2006). Exploring turnover intentions among three professional groups of employees. *Human Resource Development International, 9,* 191–206.

Chaskin, R. J. (2003). Fostering neighborhood democracy: Legitimacy and accountability within loosely coupled systems. *Nonprofit and Voluntary Sector Quarterly, 32,* 161–189.

Chetkovich, C., & Frumkin, P. (2003). Balancing margin and mission: Nonprofit competition in charitable versus fee-based programs. *Administration & Society, 35*(5), 564–596.

Cunningham, I. (2016). Non-profits and the 'hollowed out' state: The transformation of working conditions through personalizing social care services during an era of austerity. *Work, Employment and Society, 30*(4), 649–668.

Drucker, P. F. (1992). *Managing the nonprofit organization: Principles and practices.* Harper.

Faulk, L. et al. (2021). *Nonprofit trends and impacts 2021. National findings on donation trends from 2015 through 2020, diversity and representation, and first-year impacts of the COVID-19 pandemic.* Urban Institute.

Foster, M. K., & Meinhard, A. (2002). A contingency view of the responses of voluntary social service organizations in Ontario to government cutbacks. *Canadian Journal of Administrative Sciences, 19*(1), 27–41.

Frumkin, P., & Andre-Clark, A. (2000). When mission, markets, and politics collide: Values and strategy in the nonprofit human services. *Nonprofit and Voluntary Sector Quarterly, 29*(1), 141–164.

Glaeser, E. L. (2003). *The Governance of Not-for-Profit Organizations.* University of Chicago Press.

Golden-Biddle, K., GermAnn, K., Reay, T. & Procyshen, G. (2007). Creating and sustaining positive organizational relationships: A cultural perspective. In J. E. Dutton, & B. R. Ragins (Eds.), *Exploring positive relationships at work: Building a theoretical and research foundation* (pp. 289–306). Lawrence Erlbaum.

Hall, M., & K. Banting. (2000). The nonprofit sector in Canada. In K. Banting (Ed.), *The nonprofit sector in Canada: Roles and relationships* (pp. 1–28). Queen's School of Policy Studies.

Hallock, K. F. (2002). Managerial pay and governance in American nonprofits. *Industrial Relations, 41*, 377–406.

Handy, F., & Brudney, J. L. (2007). When to Use Volunteer Labour Resources? An Organizational Analysis for Nonprofit Management. *Vrijwillige Inzet Onderzocht (VIO, Netherlands) Jaargang, 4*, 91–100.

Handy, F., & Katz, E. (1998). The wage differential between nonprofit institutions and corporations: Getting more by paying less? *Journal of Comparative Economics, 26*, 246–261.

Handy, F., Mook, L., & Quarter, J. (2008). The interchangeability of paid staff and volunteers in non-profit organizations. *Nonprofit and Voluntary Sector Quarterly, 37*(1), 76–92.

Hansmann, H. B. (1980). The role of nonprofit enterprise. *The Yale Law Journal, 89*(5), 835–901.

Helmig, B., Hinz, V., & Ingerfurth, S. (2015). Valuing organizational values: Assessing the uniqueness of nonprofit values. *Voluntas, 26*(6), 2554–2580.

Herman, R. D. (2004). The future of nonprofit management. In R. D. Herman (Ed.), *The Jossey-Bass handbook of nonprofit leadership & management* (2nd ed., pp. 731–735). Jossey-Bass.

Howe, P., & McDonald, C. (2001) *Traumatic stress, turnover and peer support in child welfare*. Child Welfare League of America. http://www.cwla.org/programs/trieschman/2001fbwPhilHowe.htm. Accessed October 1, 2005.

Imagine Canada. (2020, April 15). COVID-19 threatens to devastate Canada's charities. *Imagine Canada*. https://www.imaginecanada.ca/en/360/covid-19-threatens-devastate-canadas-charities

Jansen. (2020). Sector stories: 4 ways that Covid-19 is impacting nonprofit operations. *Imagine Canada*. https://www.imaginecanada.ca/en/360/sector-stories-4-ways-covid-19-impacting-nonprofit-operations [April 15, 2020].

Jeavons, T. H. (1992). When management is the message: Relating values to management practice in nonprofit organizations. *Nonprofit Management and Leadership, 2*(4), 403–417.

Jobome, G. O. (2006). Management pay, governance and performance: The case of large UK nonprofits. *Financial Accountability and Management, 22*(4), 331–58.

Kahn, W. A. (1990). Psychological conditions of personal employee engagement and disemployee engagement at work. *Academy of Management Journal, 33*, 692–724.

Kahn, W. A. (1992). To be fully there: Psychological presence at work. *Human Relations, 45*, 321–349.

Kalleberg, A. L., Marden, P., Reynolds, J., & Knoke, D. (2006). Beyond profit! Sectoral difference in high-performance work practices. *Work and Occupations, 33*(3), 271–302.

Kim, S. (2005). Three big management challenges in nonprofit human services agencies. *International Review of Public Administration, 10*(1), 85–93.

Knutsen, W. L., & Brower, R. S. (2010). Managing expressive and instrumental accountabilities in nonprofit and voluntary organizations: A qualitative investigation. *Nonprofit and Voluntary Sector Quarterly, 39*(4), 588–610.

Liao-Troth, M. A. (2001). Attitude differences between paid workers and volunteers. *Nonprofit Management and Leadership, 11*, 423–442. https://doi.org/10.1002/nml.11403

Leete, L. (2001). Whiter the nonprofit wage differential? Estimates from the 1990 Census. *Journal of Labor Economics, 19*(1), 136–170.

LePine, J., Erez, A., & Johnson, D. (2002). The nature and dimensionality of organizational citizenship behavior: A critical review and meta-analysis. *Journal of Applied Psychology, 87*, 52–65.

Light, P. C. (2002). The content of their character: The state of the nonprofit workforce. *The Nonprofit Quarterly, 9*(3), 6–16.

Light, P. C. (2003). *The health of the human services workforce*. Brookings Institution.

Macey, W., & Schneider, B. (2008). The meaning of employee engagement. *Industrial and Organizational Psychology, 1*, 3–30.

Maulhardt, M., Smith, J., & Carpenter, T. (2015). *UST Nonprofit employee engagement & retention report: A survey of nonprofit executives, supervisors, and staff*. Unemployment Services Trust.

McDermott, A. M., Heffernan, M., & Beynon, M. J. (2013). When the nature of employment matters in the employment relationship: A cluster analysis of psychological contracts and organizational commitment in the non-profit sector. *The International Journal of Human Resource Management, 24*(7), 1490–1518.

McDonald, R. E. (2007). An investigation of innovation in nonprofit organizations: The role of organizational mission. *Nonprofit and Voluntary Sector Quarterly, 36*(2), 256–281.

McHatton, P.A., Bradshaw, W., Gallagher, P.A., & Reeves, R. (2011). Results from a strategic planning process: Benefits for a nonprofit organization. *Nonprofit Management and Leadership, 22*(2), 233–249.

McMullen, K., & Schellenberg, G. (2002). *Mapping the nonprofit sector* (No. 1). Canadian Policy Research Network.

McMullen, K., & Schellenberg, G. (2003). *Job quality in nonprofit organizations*. Canadian Policy Research Network.

Melnik, E., Petrella, F., & Richez-Battesti, N. (2013). Does the professionalism of management practices in nonprofits and for-profits affect job satisfaction? *International Journal of Human Resource Management, 24*(6), 1300–1321.

Mesch, D. J., & Rooney, P. M. (2008). Determinants of compensation: A study of pay, performance, and gender differences for fundraising professionals. *Nonprofit Management & Leadership, 18*(4), 435–463.

Meyer, J. P., & Allen, N. J. (1991). A three-component conceptualization of organizational commitment. *Human Resource Management Review, 1*, 61–89.

Meyer, J. P., Stanley, D. J., Herscovitch, L., & Topolnytsky, L. (2002). Affective, continuance, and normative commitment to the organization: A meta-analysis of antecedents, correlates, and consequences. *Journal of Vocational Behavior, 61*, 20–52.

Mogus, J., & Levihn-Coon, A. (2018, February 6). What Makes Nonprofit Digital Teams Successful Today? *Stanford Social Innovation Review.* https://ssir.org/articles/entry/what_makes_nonprofit_digital_teams_successful_today. Accessed September 28, 2018.

Moore, T., & McKee, K. (2012). "Empowering local communities? An international review of community land trusts" (Policy Review). *Housing Studies, 27*(2), 280–290.

Moore, T., & Mullins, D. (2013). Scaling-up or going viral? Comparing self-help housing and community land trust facilitation. *Voluntary Sector Review, 4*(3), 333–354.

Moulton, S., & Eckerd, A. (2012). Preserving the publicness of the nonprofit sector: Resources, roles, and public values. *Nonprofit and Voluntary Sector Quarterly, 41*(4), 656–685.

Newton, C. J., & Mazur, A. K. (2016). Value congruence and job-related attitudes in a nonprofit organization: A competing values approach. *The International Journal of Human Resource Management, 27*, 1013–1033. https://doi.org/10.1080/09585192.2015.1053962[AQ28]

O'Neill, M., & Young, D. R. (1988). Educating managers of nonprofit organizations. In M. O'Neill & D. R. Young (Eds.), *Educating managers of nonprofit organizations* (pp. 1–21). Praeger.

Organ, D. W. (1988). *Organizational citizenship behavior: The good soldier syndrome.* Lexington Books.

Park, S., Kim, J., Park, J., & Lim, D. H. (2018). Work engagement in nonprofit organizations: A conceptual model. *Human Resource Development Review, 17*, 5–33.

Parry, E., Kelliher, C., Mills, T., & Tyson, S. (2005). Comparing HRM in the voluntary and public sectors. *Personnel Review, 34*(5), 588–602.

Pichault, F., & Schoenaers, F. (2003). HRM practices in a process of organizational change: A contextual perspective. *Applied Psychology: An International Review, 52*(1), 120–143.

Putnam, R. (2000). *Bowling alone: The collapse and revival of American community*. Simon & Schuster.
Quarter, J. (1992). *Canada's social economy: Co-operatives, nonprofits and other community enterprises*. James Lorimer & Company.
Quarter, J., Mook, L., & Armstrong, A. (2009). *Understanding the social economy: A Canadian perspective*. University of Toronto Press.
Rich, B. L., Lepine, J. A., & Crawford, E. R. (2010). Job engagement: Antecedents and effects on job performance. *Academy of Management Journal, 53*, 617–635.
Ridder, H., & McCandless, A. (2010). Influences on the architecture of human resource management in nonprofit organizations: An analytical framework. *Nonprofit and Voluntary Sector Quarterly, 39*, 124–141.
Roomkin, M., & Weisbrod, B. (1999). Managerial compensation and incentives in for-profit and non-profit hospitals. *Journal of Law, Economics, and Organisations, 15*, 750–781.
Saks, A. M. (2006). Antecedents and consequences of employee engagement. *Journal of Managerial Psychology, 21*, 600–619.
Salamon, L. M., Hems, L. C., & Chinnock, K. (2000). *The nonprofit sector: For what and for whom?* (Working Papers of the Johns Hopkins Comparative Nonprofit Sector Project, no. 37). Baltimore: The Johns Hopkins Center for Civil Society Studies.
Schaufeli, W. B., Salanova, M., Gonzalez-Roma, V., & Bakker, A. B. (2002). The measurement of employee engagement and burnout: A two sample confirmatory factor analytic approach. *Journal of Happiness Studies, 3*, 71–92.
Schepers, C., De Gieter, S., Pepermans, R., Du Bois, C., Caers, R., & Jegers, M. (2005). How are employees of the nonprofit sector motivated? *Nonprofit Management & Leadership, 16*(2), 191–208.
Selander, K. (2015). Work engagement in the third sector. *VOLUNTAS: International Journal of Voluntary and Nonprofit Organizations, 26*, 1391–1411. https://doi.org/10.1007/s11266-014-9465-y
Selden, S. C., & Sowa, J. E. (2015). Voluntary turnover in nonprofit human service organizations: The impact of high performance work practices. *Human Service Organizations: Management, Leadership & Governance, 39*, 182–207.
Shier, M. L., & Handy, F. (2015). From advocacy to social innovation: A typology of social change efforts by nonprofits. *VOLUNTAS: International Journal of Voluntary and Nonprofit Organizations, 26*, 2581–2603.
Shier, M. L., Handy, F., & Jennings, C. (2018). Intraorganizational conditions supporting social innovations by human service nonprofits. *Nonprofit and Voluntary Sector Quarterly*. https://doi.org/10.1177/0899764018797477
Smith, R., & Lipsky, M. (1993). *Nonprofits for hire: The welfare state in the age of contracting*. Harvard University Press.

Shuck, B., Twyford, D., Reio, T. G., Jr., & Shuck, A. (2014). Human resource development practices and employee engagement: Examining the connection with employee turnover intentions. *Human Resource Development Quarterly, 25,* 239–270.

Steel, R. P., & Ovalle, N. K. (1984). A review of the meta-analysis of research on the relationship between behavioral intentions and employee turnover. *Journal of Applied Psychology, 69,* 673–686.

Svensson, P. G., Jeong, S., Shuck, B., & Otto, M. G. (2021). Antecedents and outcomes of employee engagement in sport for development. *Sport Management Review, 24*(4), 673–696. https://doi.org/10.1080/14413523.2021.1880758

Turkewitz, D. (2022, March 31). *Communities first: Centering service where It's needed most.* https://www.newyorkcares.org/blogs/communities-first-centering-service-where-it-s-needed-most

Udavant, S. (2022, August). Why tech nonprofits are building digital tools for racial equity and justice. *Nonprofit Quarterly.* Retrieved August 26, 2022, https://nonprofitquarterly.org/tech-noonprofits-building-digital-tools-racial-equity-racial-justice/?mc_cid=c78d7fd821&mc_eid=ade6362326

CHAPTER 3

Nonprofit Employee Engagement Model

The need for nonprofit organizations to deploy employee engagement as the core of their human resource strategy cannot be over-emphasized. In Chapter 2, we explain how the multidimensional factors of the basic characteristics of nonprofits, their operating environment, and their employees combine to influence employee engagement. We note that while the antecedents and benefits are relevant in nonprofit organizations, the distinctive multidimensional factors have been highlighted to contribute to a unique environment for employee engagement. Moreover, as Table 3.1 shows, during COVID-19 in Canada, nonprofit organizations were more likely to introduce practices that signify a supportive work environment that facilitates employee engagement than their for-profit counterparts. With the understanding of the multidimensional factors, the antecedents, and benefits of nonprofit employee engagement at the back of our minds, the logical question is, what are some of the models of employee engagement that could bring these elements together to guide the planning, implementation, and evaluation of employee engagement in a nonprofit organization.

Therefore, the goal of this chapter is to present and explain a conceptual model for effective employee engagement in nonprofit organizations. The model highlights the core components of employee engagement rather than a linear process and draws on theoretical perspectives that

© The Author(s), under exclusive license to Springer Nature Switzerland AG 2023
K. Akingbola et al., *Employee Engagement in Nonprofit Organizations*, https://doi.org/10.1007/978-3-031-08469-0_3

Table 3.1 Employee supports and COVID-19 mitigation measures

Employee supports provided due to COVID-19, which were not provided before the pandemic	Nonprofit (%)	For-profit (%)
Access to mental health services	12	5
Virtual social gatherings with work colleagues	30	11
Childcare subsidy	0.7	0.6
Family care-related leave	9	6
Paid sick leave specifically for COVID-19	18	11
Other paid or unpaid time off	22	13
Other support	16	6
None	39	68

Source Statistics Canada (2021). Summary of Findings from the Business Conditions Survey April 2021. https://www150.statcan.gc.ca/n1/daily-quotidien/210827/dq210827b-eng.htm

have been used to explain employee engagement in nonprofit organizations. The chapter starts with a brief review of two theoretical perspectives that have dominated the discourse on employee engagement: Social Exchange theory and Job Demands-Resources Model. This is followed by a review of two models that offer a conceptualization of nonprofit employee engagement with contextual factors as underlying dimensions. The chapter emphasizes the nexus between research and management practices to extend the employee engagement in nonprofit organizations.

THEORETICAL PERSPECTIVES

As should be expected, many theoretical perspectives have been used to underlie the analysis of employee engagement in empirical research and conceptual papers. Two of these theoretical perspectives, Social Exchange theory and Job Demands-Resources (JD-R) model, have gained significant traction in research and are particularly relevant in the context of nonprofit organizations.

SOCIAL EXCHANGE THEORY

Social exchange theory is predicated on undefined payback obligations in the relationship between an organization and its employees (Gould-Williams & Davies, 2005). Social exchange is characterized by a give-and-take system in which "favors that create diffuse future obligations, not precisely specified ones, and the nature of the return cannot be bargained about but must be left to the discretion of the one who makes it." (Blau, 1964, p. 3). The fundamental principle in social exchange is the norm of reciprocity of action between parties. Although there are no set contracts to define the form, time, and degree of payback obligation, there is an inherent expectation of voluntary reciprocity. The individual making the gratuitous repayment is motivated by their perception of how the organization treats them. If the perception of the employees is that the organization adopts policies and practices that signify respect, dignity, and trust, the employees will develop a feeling that they owe the organization (Akingbola, 2015). In effect, the employees will reciprocate the good deeds of the organization in their own way.

Social exchange theory has provided one of the leading theoretical underpinnings for the explanation of employee engagement and the conceptualization of new approach of the construct (Bailey et al., 2017). They noted that it is the second most widely used theoretical background in employee engagement research. According to social exchange theory, engagement results when employees have the perception that the organization supports, trusts, and is committed to them. Employees interpret the policies and practices of the organization as indicators of how much the organization values them. They rely on their perception to determine the level of trust and commitment of the organization to them. If their perception suggests that the organization values them, appreciates and recognizes their contribution, employees will develop a reciprocal obligation to deploy their physical, cognitive, and emotional energy on the job and in the organization (Akingbola, 2015; Saks, 2006). Engagement is a social exchange relationship between the organization and employees.

Multidimensional Approach

One of the main theoretical approaches has used social exchange theory to explain and extend the conceptualization of employee engagement. Saks (2006) introduced a multidimensional approach to explain what engagement is about. Saks extended the earlier explanation of engagement. Kahn's (1990) original explanation focused on the need to satisfy the self in the job role while Maslach et al.'s (2001) burnout-antithesis approach suggested that employee engagement is the positive antithesis of burnout. The multidimensional approach emphasized two related but distinct factors, job engagement, and organizational engagement (Saks,

2006). Engagement can manifest from two roles of employees, "their work role and their role as a member of their organisation" (Saks, 2019, p. 20). Job engagement is about investment of the self in the work role, while organization engagement has to do with the greater investment of the self as members of the organization (Saks, 2006; Saks & Gruman, 2014).

From its root in social exchange theory, the multidimensional approach suggests that the more support and socio-emotional resources that the organization provides to employees, the more reciprocal obligation employees will develop to invest more on the job and in the organization. Below, we provide a summary of research on nonprofit employee engagement that used social exchange theory as a theoretical approach.

Job Demands-Resources Model

Job Demands-Resources (JD-R) model is a theoretical framework that is particularly relevant for examining and understanding work behavior, employee well-being, and the characteristics of the work environment of employees. JD-R underlies the engagement as job resources perspective that we discuss in Chapter 1. The original JD-R model categorizes an extensive range of work-related factors into two categories—job demands and job resources—based on their impact on employee engagement (Demerouti et al., 2001). Job demands are the "physical, social, or organizational aspects of the job that require sustained physical and/or psychological effort or skills... and are associated with certain physiological and/or psychological costs" (Bakker & Demerouti, 2007, p. 312). Examples of the costs of job demands include emotional exhaustion and heavy workload (Demerouti et al., 2001).

On the other hand, job resources consist of the "physical, psychological, social, and organizational aspects of the job that are either functional in achieving work goals, reduce job demands and the associated physiological and psychological costs, or stimulate personal growth, learning, and development" (Bakker & Demerouti, 2007, p. 312). Job resources are elements of the job that help to mitigate job demands and their related costs. Job resources facilitate the achievement of work goals, learning, and development of employees (Bakker & Demerouti, 2007). In these processes, job resources are either extrinsic motivator or intrinsic motivator. As extrinsic motivator, job resources are focused on the demands of the job. The focus is all about getting the job done. The primary focus of intrinsic motivator is to meet the psychological needs of employees such as facilitating autonomy. There are job resources for the tasks performed on the job, the interactions embedded in work processes, and the organizational level processes and interactions. As noted in Chapter 1, examples of job resources include job autonomy, support, training, support for development, and supervisory coaching (Bakker & Bal, 2010).

As a theoretical framework, JD-R is predicated on the two underlying assumptions (a) there are job stress components in every job and (b) job stress is likely to increase when there are high job demands and job resources are limited (Bakker & Demerouti, 2007; Demerouti et al., 2001). The assumptions, the component of job demands, and job resources highlight JD-R as a theoretical framework that explains the countervailing processes involved in fostering employee well-being which is critical to employee behavior such as commitment, organizational citizenship behavior, and engagement. Research has offered revised JD-R model that extended the scope and flexibility of the model to include more diverse organizations (Schaufeli & Taris, 2014). In addition to the flexibility, the extended job resources foster engagement by energizing employee to deploy their discretionary effort.

Engagement as Job Resources

JD-R model underlies the engagement as resources perspective discussed in Chapter 1. As a theory of engagement JD-R model emphasizes that job resources are key to fostering engagement. Job resources are uniquely connected to engagement (Bakker & Demerouti, 2007). Job resources facilitate engagement through a motivational process. Job demands put the pressures of the work role on employees which if not managed effectively, could lead to exhaustion and burnout (Crawford et al., 2010). Research suggests that six job resources, job control, supervisor support, climate, innovativeness, information, and appreciation, are positively associated with engagement (Demerouti et al., 2001). When employees have a positive perception of the six job resources, they are more likely to deploy their energy and enthusiasm on the job and for the organization. We also know that engagement manifest through job resources especially because of a sense of appreciation that employee experience (Bakker et al., 2007, p. 279). Employee perception of the job resources and how the organization leveraged them are relevant in employee engagement. It is important for organizations to understand job resources and how they impact employee engagement.

Nonprofit Employment Engagement Research

Although research on employee engagement in nonprofit organizations has gained tempo in recent years, it is significantly limited. However, the growing body of research on the subject has provided valuable insight on the distinct context of employee engagement in nonprofit organizations. To illustrate the application of the two theoretical perspectives in nonprofit engagement research, we provide an overview of two empirical research that used each of the two theories. The review also provides relevant evidence to support the conceptualization of employee engagement.

Selander's Work Engagement in the Third Sector

The study by Selander (2015) was one of the early research projects that focused specifically on employee engagement in nonprofit organizations. Selander applied an extended job demands-resources (JD-R) model to examine work engagement in a sample of Finnish third-sector employees. The research examined whether the level of work engagement of third-sector employees is higher than employees generally and the antecedents of the work engagement. Selander highlighted the unique context of nonprofit organizations by extending the job demands and resources and examining factors that include public service motivation and value congruence. Figure 3.1 shows the extended JD-R model that incorporates public service motivation and value congruence of employees (Selander, 2015).

There are three significant findings from Selander's research. First, Selander found that third-sector employees generally experience higher work engagement than other employees in engagement studies. Second, the result also indicates that the higher work engagement of third-sector employees is associated with the extended job demands and job resources of the sector (Selander, 2015). Third, importantly, the result of Selander's research shows that the level of engagement of the third-sector employees is related to their public service motivation and value congruence. Selander noted that the finding indicates that "employees

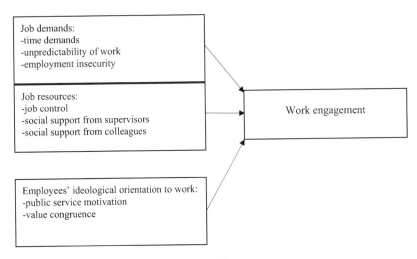

Fig. 3.1 Selander's extended JD-R model

who are motivated by public interest and share employer organization's values are more engaged in their work despite job demands and resources" (p. 1407). The findings in Selander's research are consistent with some of the multidimensional factors of nonprofit organizations and the antecedents of nonprofit employee engagement discussed in Chapter 2. Although the research did not examine the consequences of engagement, the application of the extended JD-R model and the importance of value congruence offer relevant insights into the dimensions of employee engagement.

Akingbola and van den Berg's Nonprofit Employee Engagement

The question of nonprofit employee engagement was also the focus of the research by Akingbola and van den Berg (2019). The research draws on Kahn's (1990) theory of job engagement, and Saks' (2006) multidimensional approach, to examine the relationship between antecedents and consequences of employee engagement in a sample of Canadian nonprofit employees. As noted above, Saks multidimensional approach drew on social exchange theory for theoretical background. In addition, consistent with Akingbola (2013), Akingbola and van den Berg (2019) suggested that there is a distinctive system of social exchange at play in nonprofit organizations. They extended the multidimensional approach by using measures that explain the unique context of nonprofit organizations. The measures examined the antecedents and consequences of employee engagement that consisted of both job and organization engagement. Figure 3.2 presents the model that examined the multidimensional relationship between antecedents, consequences, and employee engagement.

The findings from Akingbola and van den Berg's research point to a strong relationship between the antecedents and consequences of employee engagement in nonprofit organizations. They demonstrated that irrespective of the antecedents, nonprofit employees are more likely to experience the consequences of engagement such as job satisfaction, organizational citizenship behavior, and less likely to have intention to quit (Akingbola & van den Berg, 2019). The research also highlights several major findings. First, the effect of organization engagement was stronger than the effect of job engagement for most of the consequences. This suggests the importance of mission attachment and value congruence of nonprofit employees. Second, job characteristics are related to job engagement and rewards and recognition is associated with organization engagement. This finding reinforces the unique characteristics of nonprofit employees in terms of their social exchange expectation of trust, fairness, and respect in the policies and practices of the organization. Third, the strong relationship between organization engagement and intention to quit is an important reminder of the role of employee

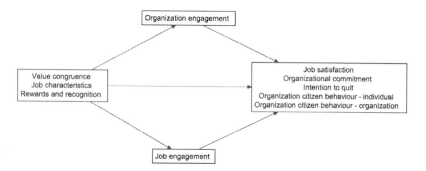

Fig. 3.2 Akingbola and van den Berg's model of antecedents and consequences with organization and job engagement mediators

engagement in retention. Fourth, together, the findings emphasize the critical importance of meaningfulness in nonprofit employee engagement. The mission attachment and value congruence signify the opportunity employees have to actualize the self through the organization. The role of organization engagement from the finding is particularly instructive about the confluence of multidimensional nonprofit factors that shape employee engagement.

In addition to the research by Selander (2015) and Akingbola and van den Berg (2019), other studies have offered valuable insights on relevant questions pertaining to nonprofit employee engagement (see. Johansen & Sowa, 2019; Park et al, 2018; Svensson et al., 2021). Park et al., (2018) specifically proposed a conceptual model of work engagement in nonprofit organizations that used a revised JD-R model. Their model reiterates the findings of the research by Selander (2015) and the relevance of the JD-R model in nonprofit employee engagement.

Nonprofit Employee Engagement Model

The summary of the findings from Selander (2015) and Akingbola and van den Berg (2019) incorporate the dimensions of the contextual factors that underlie nonprofit employee engagement. Moreover, both research studies adopted the two primary theoretical perspectives that have been used to explain employee engagement. By extending JD-R and social exchange theories to include factors that are unique to nonprofits, Selander (2015) and Akingbola and van den Berg (2019) offer validated theoretical underpinning for developing a conceptual model of nonprofit employee engagement.

Antecedents and Outcomes of Employee Engagement in Nonprofit Organizations

In this section, we combine the extended JD-R model, social exchange theory, and research on employee engagement in nonprofit organizations discussed above and in Chapter 2 to offer an integrated conceptual model of nonprofit employee engagement with the contextual factors as underlying factors. As highlighted in the models reviewed above, employee engagement is inextricably linked to the multidimensional factors of nonprofit organizations that consist of the environment, characteristics of nonprofits, and their employees. Therefore, the conceptual model must

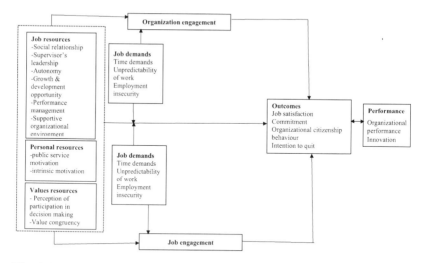

Fig. 3.3 Integrated nonprofit employee engagement model

align the multidimensional factors in nonprofit management practices to facilitate effective employee engagement. The model emphasizes the application of research in nonprofit employee engagement to enhance employee and organizational outcomes in nonprofit organizations.

Figure 3.3 shows the conceptual model of employee engagement in a nonprofit organization. Drawing on research, multidimensional factors of nonprofits, the extended JD-R model, and social exchange theory, we discuss the following components of the antecedents and outcomes of employee engagement in nonprofit organizations.

Antecedents of Nonprofit Employee Engagement

The available research has provided evidence of the impact of the antecedents identified in the integrated model of employee engagement in nonprofit organizations (Akingbola & van den Berg, 2019; Park et al., 2018; Selander, 2015).

Job Resources

Research has indicated that job resources are related to higher level of employee engagement (Selander, 2015). The role of leadership as job resources to facilitate employee engagement in nonprofit organizations is especially evidenced in research (Selander, 2015; Park et al., 2018). *Social support from supervisors* is positively related to work environment (Selander, 2015). This suggests that the encouragement, support, and other positive interactions between the employee and supervisor contribute to the higher level of engagement of the employee. Also, *transformational leadership* and modeling exemplary leadership behaviors were found to be positively related to employee engagement (de Oliveira & da Silva, 2015; Gözükara & Şimşek, 2015; Sarti, 2014). Similarly, supervisors providing performance feedback also contributed to work engagement (Miner et al., 2015). Surprisingly, as Park et al. (2018) noted, when employees' autonomy was examined as part of job resources, the evidence suggests that the findings were inconsistent in the available research. One study reported a positive relationship with work engagement while another study indicated that autonomy did not affect work engagement.

Beyond leadership and performance feedback, work engagement was also related to *job control* which signals that giving employees opportunities to determine how they do their job, use their skills, and plan their schedules, can make them to be more engaged (Selander, 2015). Work engagement was related to learning opportunities that employees have in the nonprofit organization (Sarti, 2014). This is consistent with the nonprofit focus on training and development as an important component of its human resources strategy (Akingbola, 2015). However, the relationship between high performance work systems (HPWS) and work engagement was also mixed. Although HPWS is related to work engagement (de Oliveira & da Silva, 2015), one study found different impacts of engagement on different categories of employees in a nonprofit hospital setting (Johansen & Sowa, 2019). Together, the job resources are important in shaping employee engagement in different nonprofit settings.

Personal Resources
As explained in Chapter 2, the personal resources of an employee include individual characteristics such as attitude, personality, behavior, and lived experiences. In nonprofit engagement research, these are measured in terms of public service motivation (mission attachment) and intrinsic motivation. Research evidence is consistent that public service motivation is associated with employee engagement (Akingbola & van den Berg,

2019; Selander, 2015). Public service motivation indicates a strong bond between the employee and the organization that may be explained in terms of organization engagement rather than work engagement. Intrinsic motivation is also particularly relevant in influencing employee engagement in nonprofit organizations. The perception of nonprofit employees in terms of greater opportunity for intrinsic motivation is related to engagement (Akingbola & van den Berg, 2019; Svensson et al., 2021). Nonprofit employees expect their intrinsic motivation to be actualized through the services, policies, and practices of the nonprofit organization.

Value-Based Resources
Related to the importance of mission attachment is the shared values or value congruency between employees and nonprofit organizations. Value congruence is factor in the recruitment, motivation, and retention of nonprofit employees (Brown & Yoshioka, 2003; Newton & Mazur, 2016). It is therefore not a surprise that research has indicated that value congruence is related to employee engagement (Akingbola & van den Berg, 2019; Selander, 2015). The value congruence between employees and nonprofit organization has been shown to be a particularly strong influence on the level of engagement of employees. Irrespective of job demands and resources, employees who share values of the organization are more engaged (Selander, 2015). Value congruence is a factor in the performance of nonprofit organizations because it connects employees to the core components of the nonprofit including strategy.

Employees' expectation of participation in decision-making is the second indicator of value-based resources. The expectation is tied to the perception that nonprofit organizations are egalitarian entities that would practice participatory decision-making (Brandel, 2001; Frumkin & Andre-Clerk, 2000). Therefore, when this expectation is consistent with the practice of the organization, employees are more likely to be engaged (Román-Calderón et al., 2013). The positive relationship between engagement and participation in decision-making supports the practices of nonprofits that generally provide employees the opportunity to participate in decision-making.

Job Demands
The challenges of nonprofit organizations are extensive. This suggests that the work environment of nonprofits is characterized by job demands

factors such as time demands, unpredictability of work, and employment insecurity. The unpredictability of funding and precarious employment due to shifting regulatory demands are particularly challenging to nonprofit organizations and their employees (Cunningham, 2016). Research has shown that time demands have a negative impact on employee engagement while unpredictability of work decreases engagement (Selander, 2015). However, the research found that employment insecurity is not related to employee engagement. The findings suggest that while time demands negatively impact engagement, public service motivation, and value congruence mitigate its impact. Selander (2015) opined that unpredictability of work is a major concern for nonprofit employees than job insecurity.

Outcomes of Nonprofit Employee Engagement

The outcomes of employee engagement signify not only the benefits of the construct for the organization but also for the engaged employees. Therefore, each of the outcomes has implications for employees and the organization. Although nonprofit organizations potentially benefits significantly from a high level of employee engagement, research is yet to examine many of the possible benefits. Below, we provide a summary of the outcomes from available research.

Job Satisfaction
Nonprofit employees who are engaged are more likely to experience job satisfaction (Akingbola & van den Berg, 2019). The research indicates that the characteristics of nonprofit jobs contribute to job satisfaction which further highlights the importance of mission alignment in employee engagement.

Commitment
Due to their attachment to the mission and values of the organization, nonprofit employees are known to have an inherent commitment to the nonprofits. Research has found that engagement also contributes to the commitment of nonprofit employees (Akingbola & van den Berg, 2019). Both job and organization engagement mediate the impact of antecedent factors on commitment. Engagement contributes to enhance the level of

commitment that employees already have in the organization. Engagement is a value-added enhancing process that nonprofits can deploy to further the commitment of their employees.

Organizational Citizenship Behavior (OCB)
OCB has been identified as one of the outcomes of employee engagement in nonprofit organizations. The research found that OCB is related to employee engagement in nonprofit organizations (Akingbola & van den Berg, 2019; Park et al., 2018). The social exchange appears to be an important factor in the relationship between engagement and OCB of nonprofit employees. Since employees expect nonprofits to exemplify the values they espouse in their policies and practices, engaged employees are therefore likely to have a positive experience that indicates the use of the espoused values. They are therefore more likely to develop reciprocal obligation that is demonstrated through OCB. In effect, engagement will tend to result in voluntary behavior such as helpfulness, conscientiousness, and civic virtue.

Intention to Quit
A high level of employee turnover is a concern in any organization. Intension to quit is a reliable predictor of employee turnover (Steel & Ovalle, 1984). Therefore, the intention to quit is a major concern for nonprofit organizations. However, employee engagement is one of the ways to mitigate the challenges of the intention to quit. Research has provided evidence of this relationship. The research suggests that employee engagement is positively related to the intention to quit in nonprofit organizations (Akingbola & van den Berg, 2019; Park et al., 2018; Svensson et al., 2021). The research suggests that engaged employees are less likely to indicate that they have an intention to quit. As noted above, the finding from the research emphasizes that irrespective of antecedents, engagement has direct impact on intention to quit in nonprofit organizations (Akingbola & van den Berg, 2019). Engagement is an important process that can be deployed to address employee turnover in nonprofit organizations.

Organizational Performance and Innovation

Organizational performance is multidimensional and is generally relative to the unique services of the nonprofit organization (Herman, &

Renz, 1997). Consistent with the social mission of nonprofit organizations, performance is social in nature. It is qualitative and not easy to measure. Moreover, the mission that represents the core purpose of the nonprofit organization is intended to communicate the public good that the organization is established to achieve and the people the organization intends to serve. The mission is important to attract the resources that the organization needs for service delivery, management, and governance including employees, volunteers, and funders (Bradach et al., 2008). What is measured as performance, the way it is measured and reported, therefore depends on the perception of the stakeholders.

The point of this brief discussion on nonprofit performance is to highlight why organizational performance is yet to be examined in the research on employee engagement in nonprofit organizations. Although a recent study included performance as an antecedent of employee engagement, the research is based on the perception of performance. We have therefore included organizational performance as an outcome variable in the proposed model of employee engagement in a nonprofit organization to provide a theoretical basis for the analysis of performance in future research.

Conclusion

This chapter offers a conceptual model of employee engagement in nonprofit organizations. The model integrates the multidimensional factors that underlie the organization with the theoretical perspectives of JD-R and social exchange theory as well as research on employee engagement in nonprofit organizations. The conceptual model also provides a framework to guide nonprofit organizations that want to implement a model that is consistent with their operating environment. The overview of the two research perspectives highlights the core components of employee engagement rather than a linear process and draws on theoretical perspectives that have been used to explain employee engagement in nonprofit organizations.

Discussion Questions

1. Describe the revised JD-R model that included nonprofit factors
2. How would you explain the differences between job and organization engagement in the context of nonprofit organizations?

3. Is a conceptual model of nonprofit employee engagement necessary? Why can't nonprofits use the same model as organizations in other sectors?
4. What are the main findings of Selander's (2015) research?
5. What are the main findings of Akingbola and van den Berg's (2019) research?

References

Akingbola, K. (2013). Context and nonprofit human resource management. *Administration & Society, 45*, 974–1004.

Akingbola, K. (2015). *Managing human resources for nonprofits*. Routledge.

Akingbola, K., & van den Berg, H. A. (2019). Antecedents, consequences, and context of employee engagement in nonprofit organizations. *Review of Public Personnel Administration, 39*(1), 46–74. https://doi.org/10.1177/0734371X16684910

Bailey, C., Madden, A., Alfes, K., & Fletcher, L. (2017). The meaning, antecedents and outcomes of employee engagement: A narrative synthesis. *International Journal of Management Reviews, 19*(1), 31–53.

Bakker, A. B., & Bal, M. P. (2010). Weekly work employee engagement and performance: A study among starting teachers. *Journal of Occupational and Organizational Psychology, 83*(1), 189–206. https://doi.org/10.1348/096317909X402596

Bakker, A. B., & Demerouti, E. (2007). The job demands-resources model: State of the art. *Journal of Managerial Psychology, 22*(3), 309–328. https://doi.org/10.1108/02683940710733115

Bakker, A. B., Hakanen, J. J., Demerouti, E., & Xanthopoulou, D. (2007). Job resources boost work engagement, particularly when job demands are high. *Journal of Educational Psychology, 99*(2), 274–284.

Blau, P. (1964). *Exchange and power in social life*. Wiley.

Bradach, J. L., Tierney, T. J., & Stone, N. (2008, December). Delivering on the promise of nonprofits. *Harvard Business Review*.

Brandel, G. A. (2001). The truth about working in not-for-profit. *CPA Journal, 71*(10), 13.

Brown, W. A., & Yoshioka, C. (2003). Mission attachment and satisfaction as factors in employee retention. *Nonprofit Leadership and Management, 14*(1), 5–18.

Crawford, E. R., LePine, J. A., & Rich, B. L. (2010). Linking job demands and resources to employee engagement and burnout: A theoretical extension and meta-analytic test. *Journal of Applied Psychology,* 95(5), 834–848. https://doi.org/10.1037/a0019364

Cunningham, I. (2016). Non-profits and the 'hollowed out' state: The transformation of working conditions through personalizing social care services during an era of austerity. *Work, Employment and Society,* 30(4), 649–668.

de Oliveira, L. B., & da Silva, F. F. R. A. (2015). The effects of high performance work systems and leader-member exchange quality on employee engagement: Evidence from a Brazilian non-profit organization. *Procedia Computer Science,* 55, 1023–1030. https://doi.org/10.1016/j.procs.2015.07.092

Demerouti, E., Bakker, A. B., Nachreiner, F., Schaufeli, W. B. (2001, June). The job demands-resources model of burnout. *Journal of Applied Psychology,* 86(3), 499–512. PMID: 11419809.

Frumkin, P., & Andre-Clark, A. (2000). When mission, markets, and politics collide: Values and strategy in the nonprofit human services. *Nonprofit and Voluntary Sector Quarterly,* 29(1), 141–164.

Gould-Williams, J., & Davies, F. (2005). Using social exchange theory to predict the effects of HRM practice on employee outcomes. *Public Management Review,* 7(1), 1–24.

Gözükara, İ., & Şimşek, O. F. (2015). Linking transformational leadership to work engagement and the mediator effect of job autonomy: A study in a Turkish private non-profit university. *Procedia—Social and Behavioral Sciences,* 195, 963–971. https://doi.org/10.1016/j.sbspro.2015.06.274

Herman, R. D., & Renz, D. O. (1997). Multiple constituencies and the social construction of nonprofit organization effectiveness. *Nonprofit and Voluntary Sector Quarterly,* 26(2), 185–206.

Johansen, M. S., & Sowa, J. E. (2019). Human resource management, employee engagement, and nonprofit hospital performance. *Nonprofit Management and Leadership,* 29(4), 549–567.

Kahn, W. A. (1990). Psychological conditions of personal employee engagement and employee engagement at work. *Academy of Management Journal,* 33, 692–724.

Maslach, C., Schaufeli, W., & Leiter, M. (2001). Job burnout. *Annual Review of Psychology,* 52, 397–422.

Miner, M. H., Bickerton, G., Dowson, M., & Sterland, S. (2015). Spirituality and work engagement among church leaders. *Mental Health, Religion & Culture,* 18, 57–71. https://doi.org/10.1080/13674676.2014.1003168

Newton, C. J., & Mazur, A. K. (2016). Value congruence and job-related attitudes in a nonprofit organization: A competing values approach. *The International Journal of Human Resource Management,* 27, 1013–1033. https://doi.org/10.1080/09585192.2015.1053962

Park, S., Kim, J., Park, J., & Lim, D. H. (2018). Work engagement in nonprofit organizations: A conceptual model. *Human Resource Development Review, 17*, 5–33.

Román-Calderón, J. P., Battistelli, A., & Odoardi, C. (2013). Work engagement as mediator between perceived participation, supervisor support and altruistic behaviors: Empirical results from the Italian social enterprise sector. *Universitas Psychologica, 12*, 899–909.

Saks, A. M. (2006). Antecedents and consequences of employee engagement. *Journal of Managerial Psychology, 21*(7), 600–619.

Saks, A. M. (2019). Antecedents and consequences of employee engagement revisited. *Journal of Organizational Effectiveness: People and Performance, 6*(1), 19–38.

Saks, A. M., & Gruman, J. A. (2011). Manage employee engagement to manage performance. *Industrial and Organizational Psychology, 4*(2), 204–207.

Saks, A. M., & Gruman, J. A. (2014). What do we really know about employee engagement? *Human Resource Development Quarterly, 25*(2), 155–182.

Sarti, D. (2014). Job resources as antecedents of engagement at work: Evidence from a longterm care setting. *Human Resource Development Quarterly, 25*, 213–237. https://doi.org/10.1002/hrdq.21189

Schaufeli, W. B., & Bakker, A. B. (2004). Job demands, job resources, and their relationship with burnout and engagement: A multi- sample study. *Journal of Organizational Behavior: The International Journal of Industrial, Occupational and Organisational Psychology and Behavior, 25*(3), 293–315.

Schaufeli, W. B., & Taris, T. W. (2014). A critical review of the job demands-resources model: Implications for improving work and health. In G. F. Bauer & O. Hämmig (Eds.), *Bridging occupational, organizational and public health: A transdisciplinary approach* (pp. 43–68). Springer.

Selander, K. (2015). Work engagement in the third sector. *VOLUNTAS: International Journal of Voluntary and Nonprofit Organizations, 26*(4), 1391–1411. https://doi.org/10.1007/s11266-014-9465-y

Steel, R. P., & Ovalle, N. K. (1984). A review of the meta-analysis of research on the relationship between behavioral intentions and employee turnover. *Journal of Applied Psychology, 69*(4), 673–686.

Svensson, P. G., Jeong, S., Shuck, B., & Otto, M. G. (2021). Antecedents and outcomes of employee engagement in sport for development. *Sport Management Review, 24*(4), 673–696. https://doi.org/10.1080/14413523.2021.1880758

CHAPTER 4

Creating and Sustaining Employee Engagement Through Human Resource Management

Employee engagement is far and away one of the most popular topics when it comes to managing organizations and leading people. Leading management consulting organizations have defined employee engagement as peoples' "involvement and enthusiasm...in both their work and workplace" (Harter et al., 2020a) and their "attachment to the [organization] and willingness to give discretionary effort". In the academic literature, Rich et al. (2010) define engagement as the "investment of an individual's physical, cognitive, and emotional energy in...work performance" (p. 619), while Schaufeli et al. (2002) describe it as an employee state of mind that is filled with vigor, dedication, and absorption at work. The opposite, employee disengagement, involves a person's decision to withdraw themselves physically, intellectually, and/or emotionally while working (Kahn, 1990).

One reason for such strong interest in employee engagement is the so-called "business case" associated with having engaged employees. A 2020 meta-analysis[1] of the relationship between employee engagement and workplace outcomes revealed that engagement is significantly statistically correlated with a host of individual and organizational performance indicators. In organizations where engagement is higher, worker turnover

---

[1] A meta-analysis is comprehensive statistical analysis of the results of many other individual studies.

and absenteeism rates are lower, customer and client loyalty is enhanced, a greater proportion of employees is thriving and report more well-being, and productivity and production quality rise (Harter et al., 2020b). Additionally, findings from a 2019 global study conducted by professional consulting and advisory firm WTW (formerly Willis Towers Watson) on the effects of employee engagement across 41 multinational companies revealed that organizations with more engaged workers experienced up to five times sales growth and half the number of workplace safety incidents and injuries.

Within nonprofit and service organizations specifically, employee engagement has also been shown to markedly improve internal and external success. A 12-month survey of over 95 U.S. nonprofit, philanthropic, and civic and social organizations conducted by the employee experience platform company Culture Amp found that engaged employees are more emotionally connected to their organizations, have longer tenures, are less likely to quit, and are more productive and effective in their work. Using a sample of Canadian nonprofits, Akingbola and van den Berg (2019) demonstrate that employee engagement leads to increased job satisfaction, organizational commitment, and organizational citizenship behavior (that is, one's performance of workplace helping behaviors that go above and beyond their job duties and responsibilities, and which directly benefit coworkers and the organization). And drawing on a study of nonprofit hospitals, Johansen and Sowa (2019) found that higher levels of employee engagement were associated with lower hospital readmission rates and increased managerial and patient perceptions of hospital performance and service quality. There is plenty of evidence confirming the link between employee engagement and positive individual and organizational outcomes.

The Role of Job Demands and Resources in Engagement

The question for nonprofit leaders and organizations, then, becomes how to develop and maintain an engaged workforce. In this chapter, we attempt to answer this important question by using a human resource management approach. Employee engagement does not happen by chance. Instead, it emerges as a result of specific workforce and organizational dynamics. And those engagement-enhancing dynamics can be built, modulated, and sustained through the strategic and skillful use of human resource management. As an organizing framework for this chapter, we utilize the Job Demands and Resources (JD-R) model to introduce several key engagement-related organizational themes—work–life balance, employee health and wellness, flexible work arrangements, role clarity, supervisor and coworker social support, and employee perceptions of organizational fairness and their level of trust in senior organization leadership—and then discuss how nonprofit organizations and leaders can leverage HR practices to maximize the dynamics in these themes and create engaged workforces.

The JD-R model is perhaps the most commonly-used theoretical and academic approach to the study of employee engagement. In a 2022 review of job engagement research, Saks noted that "research on the predictors or antecedents of employee engagement has been primarily based on the Job Demands-Resources (JD-R) model" (p. 2). The JD-R was first introduced by Demerouti et al. (2001), and since that time numerous scholarly articles, chapters, and books have explained, tested, and advanced its understanding. The job demands and resources approach to employee engagement basically argues that workers encounter all sorts of job demands—workload, time pressures, interpersonal conflicts at work, employment insecurity, lack of clear guidance, difficult bosses, and so on—that threaten to burn them out. And if they reach burnout, disengagement and negative individual and organizational outcomes will follow. Two ways to head off this burnout-disengagement-negativity cycle are to reduce job demands *and* increase job resources. Decreasing job demands means doing things like establishing reasonable and manageable workloads or eliminating abusive supervision. Increasing job resources means doing things like creating an organizational climate where everyone feels like part of a team and is willing to help one another, providing employee training and leadership development opportunities that stimulate growth and personal learning, and allowing employees to participate in organizational decision-making.

In a summary of the theory by one of its earliest researchers, Schaufeli (2017) explains that the JD-R model combines two key psychological processes—stress and motivation—to explain the effects of job characteristics on employee experience. About these two processes, he notes:

> First, a *stress* process, which is sparked by excessive job demands and lacking resources may...lead to negative outcomes. Essentially, when job demands (the 'bad things') are chronically high and not compensated

by job resources (the 'good things'), employee's energy is progressively drained. This may finally result in a state of mental exhaustion ('burnout'), which, in its turn, may lead to negative outcomes for the individual (e.g., poor health) as well as for the organization (e.g., poor performance). Second, a *motivational* process, which is triggered by abundant job resources...may...lead to positive outcomes. Job resources (the 'good things')...spark employee's energy and make them feel engaged. (p. 121)

Importantly, Scahufeli (2017) clarifies that "only abundant job resources (and *not* low job demands) contribute to work engagement" (p. 121). Recall that the JD-R model includes two psychological processes, a stress process (which leads to burnout) and a motivation process (which leads to engagement). Job demands relate to stress and burnout, whereas job resources relate both to stress and burnout (by lowering stress and thus preventing burnout) *and* motivation and engagement (by sparking excitement and energy among employees). The practical implication of this for nonprofit organizations is that leaders must not only focus on easing work demands, which is arguably the easier of the two tasks. Leaders may be tempted to believe that their work is done after addressing a few demand-related organizational issues here and there. Instead, for employee engagement to truly take hold, nonprofits must also proactively develop and continually deliver job resources to workers.

Plainly put, workers need appropriate resources to be able to do their jobs and perform work well. These resources can be physical (e.g., a safe working environment or certain computer technologies), psychological (e.g., the "psychological safety" [Kahn, 1990] to try new things at work, make mistakes sometimes, and learn), social (e.g., feedback from one's supervisor or support from coworkers), or organizational (e.g., pay levels, job security, or work design). When people do not have the resources they need, they become burned out and disengaged from their work and organizations. Conversely, when they have abundant resources, they become motivated, energized, and engaged.

CREATING AND SUSTAINING ENGAGEMENT THROUGH JOB RESOURCE-ENHANCING HUMAN RESOURCE PRACTICES

We now focus our attention on several job-related resources that have been shown to enhance engagement: work–life balance, employee health and wellness, flexible work arrangements, role clarity, supervisor and coworker social support, and employee perceptions of organizational fairness and their level of trust in senior organizational leadership. While we will necessarily sometimes touch job demands (or the "bad things" as Schaufeli describes them) during our treatment of job resources, we purposefully take a positive approach and home in on the "good things" managers can do to spark worker energy and positivity. This is because, as Schaufeli (2017) contends, increasing job resources *both* prevents burnout *and* fosters employee engagement, whereas reducing job demands may prevent burnout but does not guarantee engagement. In presenting each job resource, we first discuss its relation to the employee experience, and then we describe how nonprofit leaders can leverage human resource practices to foster employee engagement.

Work–Life Balance

What can nonprofit organizations, leaders, and managers do to help employees feel genuinely supported and appreciated? Professor Alan Saks of the University of Toronto proffers a conceptual model whereby a system of "caring human resources management" practices can lead to employee engagement (Saks, 2022). One of these caring HR practices includes establishing work–life balance initiatives. The point that employees want to feel cared for by their work organizations is so seemingly simple and obvious that it runs the risk of being ignored or even forgotten by nonprofit organizations and leaders. Indeed, surveys of workers suggest that employers are largely not tending to employee needs for care, concern, and support. A February 2022 Gallup survey of more than 15,000 U.S. employees found that fewer than one in four felt strongly that their employer cared about their well-being (Harter, 2022). This is a huge missed opportunity for leaders and organizations since those who *do* feel strongly cared for and supported by their employers are 71% less likely to experience burnout, 69% less likely to be actively looking for a new job, and 36% more likely to feel as though they are thriving in their overall lives. These same individuals are also five times more likely to advocate for their organization and to trust the organization and its leadership and are 300% more engaged at work!

Work–life balance, which is sometimes called work–family balance or quality of work–life (QWL), has been defined as "an individual's ability to meet both their work and family commitments, as well as other non-work responsibilities and activities" (Parkes & Langford, 2008). A healthy balance between an employee's work and non-work responsibilities is beneficial for their own health and well-being as well as that of their families (Eby et al., 2005; Pocock, 2003) and is related to lower employee stress and higher satisfaction (Allen et al., 2000). Work–life balance has also been shown to correlate negatively with depression and anxiety (Haar et al., 2014). When people feel a sense of balance between work and nonwork demands, they perform their jobs better, are more committed to their work organizations, and are less likely to quit (Wayne et al., 2004). Conversely, a lack of work–life balance results in employee burnout and disengagement (Halsbeleben, 2010).

Nonprofit organizations can enhance workforce engagement by demonstrating authentic care and concern for employee demands outside of work, such as parental or elder care responsibilities, and taking tangible steps to support the interface of life inside and outside of work. The Canadian Centre for Occupational Health and Safety provides several possible human resource management interventions, including on-site, emergency, and seasonal childcare programs; eldercare initiatives such as referral programs, eldercare assessment, and case management; parental and family leave policies; on-site and external educational and training opportunities; and vacation and leave policies such as sabbaticals, community service leaves, educational leaves, and other organization-funded or self-funded leaves that allow for employee self-development and rest.

Employee Health and Wellness

There are clear linkages between a workforce's physical and mental health and wellness, and employee engagement and organizational success. Healthy employees have higher work performance and report a higher overall quality of life (Harvard Business Review Analytic Services, 2013; Institute for Health and Productivity Studies, 2015). Additionally, employees who participate in employer-sponsored health promotion and management programs (such as stress management education, health risk appraisals, nutrition classes, accident prevention activities, and so on) tend to have higher job satisfaction, are absent from work less frequently, have lower turnover rates, and incur fewer injuries and lower workers' compensation costs (Bernacki & Baun, 1984; Breslow et al., 1990; Golaszewski et al., 1992; Shephard, 1992).

Caring organizations can proactively drive up employee engagement by conducting HR practices that promote worker health and well-being, such as creating organization-wide wellness policies or implementing healthy living programs and initiatives. One U.S. Centers for Disease Control and Prevention (CDC) website categorizes employer-initiated health and wellness offerings into three types: wellness events, services, and resources. Wellness events might include fitness and exercise programs, nutrition fairs, walks, or resilience programs, among others. Services might range from screening to coaching to counseling to cessation programs and others. And resources refer to the provision of on-site and virtual learning programs and training as well as referrals to external support providers and agencies.

In terms of actually creating and maintaining an organizational health and wellness strategy, the following practical considerations and action steps can help to ensure program effectiveness and success:

- **Conducting assessments** that allow the organization to accurately measure: (1) employee health and wellness needs and wants, (2) the legality and regulatory requirements of any program or initiative to be considered, (3) what internal and external resources are available for health promotion, and (4) the costs and benefits of program implementation,
- **Obtaining organizational leadership support and buy-in** by clearly articulating how health and wellness initiatives support short- and long-term strategic priorities,
- **Getting input and ground-up support from employees** about the creation, design, and development of wellness programs and initiatives,
- **Developing goals and objectives** that help develop an organizational culture of health and wellness, and that enable both employees and the organization to understand the benefits of program investment and participation,
- **Projecting a budget** that meets the needs of planned health promotion activities but that also realistically reflects the organization's financial capabilities,
- **Carefully selecting which wellness elements to pursue**—such as stress reduction programs, health screenings, nutrition education,

smoking cessation programs, health risk assessments, and so on—and designing them in ways that reflect employee needs and desires as well as organization resources,
- **Communicating the organization's chosen health promotion strategy and objectives to all employees**, clearly articulating the benefits of participation to individuals and the organization, and
- **Periodically measuring program performance and effectiveness** using individual and organizational metrics, such as participation rates, completion rates, changes in health-related behaviors and outcomes, reduction in healthcare costs, and even increased employee morale, loyalty, commitment, and satisfaction.

Flexible Work Arrangements

The COVID-19 global pandemic brought the importance of workplace flexibility front and center for just about every work organization in the world. While there were some work organizations that explored and found ways to extend flexibility for some workers prior to COVID-19, many if not most employers in most employment sectors held to more traditional, place-based notions of work. Results from McKinsey and Company's, 2022 American Opportunity Survey, as well as from research conducted by S&P 500 member and global consulting firm Gartner, suggest that the future world of work will look and feel much different than what most people were used to prior to 2020. As the McKinsey report notes, "flexible work is no longer a temporary pandemic response but an enduring feature of the modern working world."

Based on a sample of 25,000 American workers across all sectors and geographies and representing both "blue collar" and "white collar" jobs, McKinsey's study revealed that as of spring 2022, 23% of respondents had the opportunity to work remotely on a part-time basis or occasionally, while another 35% had been offered the option of working remotely on a full-time basis. Extrapolating from the survey's representative sample, this equates to 92 million Americans now having the option to perform all or some of their work from home or remotely. Notably, the study found that when workers are given the chance to have a flexible work arrangement, nearly 9 in 10 workers take advantage of it. Eighty million Americans are doing some form of flexible work according to their estimates. McKinsey describes this finding as a "tectonic shift in where, when, and how Americans want to work."

Management consulting giant Gartner similarly chronicles changes in employee expectations about hybrid and remote work. Researchers there argue that a new "employee value proposition" which accounts for these expectation shifts is needed and will differentiate organizations that become "employers of choice" in the future world of work (Gartner, 2022). Where one works (on-site or remotely) is not the only factor that affects perceive flexibility, according to their research. A shorter work week or reduced working hours are also important considerations in the changing employee value proposition. Without these and other possibilities being given serious consideration, Gartner contends that employee engagement will suffer and attrition will result. Evidence from organization studies scholarship supports this contention. Bal and DeLange (2015) found that workplace flexibility in the form of being able to decide work schedules, starting and stopping times, and other job characteristics are positively related to employee engagement and job performance. And in a study involving nearly 775 retail workers, Moen et al. (2011) found that shifting from a time-focused working environment to one that was more focused on results and productivity (allowing workers to choose how they spent their time in pursuit of such) reduced turnover by 45.5%.

So, what can nonprofit organizations and leaders do to enable workplace flexibility? Many prospective HR practices for introducing flexible work arrangements are similar to those described above concerning work–life balance. However, one important difference here is that growing calls for employment flexibility are not necessarily tied to balancing personal demands outside of the workplace. It is not so much about giving workers space to handle non-work responsibilities as it is allowing people control over how they perform their jobs and how they contribute to organizational objectives. Workers are becoming less tolerant of an employment system solely focused on "clocking in" and that is overly concerned with meeting standard time and place prescriptions. Instead, more and more employees desire a sharper focus by employers on how their work is accomplished and the outcomes of their workplace contributions. Some engagement-enhancing HR practices that can help bring workplace flexibility to the fore include remote or hybrid work, flextime or variable working time agreements, compressed work weeks (such as four 10-hour days instead of five 8-hour days), basing working efforts and hours around job tasks and deliverables rather than duration minimums, shift and break arrangements, and job sharing, among others. A manager's ability to do some of these will be guided, and possibly limited, by labor regulations. For example, overtime regulations may constrain the extent to which employee breaks or total working hours can be adjusted. Nevertheless, nonprofit leaders stand to enhance employee engagement through thoughtful exploration of flexible work arrangement possibilities.

Role Clarity

Employees are best positioned to thrive when they have a clear understanding about their own role within an organization and what is expected of them at work. According to Zheng et al. (2016), role clarity enables one to become more confident in their abilities and decreases uncertainty about their performance potential. As a job resource, role clarity not only involves organizations being clear with employees about the nature of the tasks, duties, and responsibilities or the work to be done but also transparency and communication between managers and employees as to what workplace behaviors are expected and what does and does not constitute job performance and success (Frögéli et al., 2019). In the absence of role clarity, job demands such as role ambiguity and role conflict surface and eventually take a leading role, employees lose confidence in their abilities and become frustrated with the work environment, and burnout and disengagement potentially ensue.

Nonprofit leaders can utilize multiple HR interventions to promote role clarity and head off role ambiguity and conflict. Carefully crafted job descriptions and job specifications are an important early step. This means much more than merely tending to how job descriptions are written. When jobs are envisioned and created in the first place, the process of job analysis can help align positions to the organization's strategic objectives and set the stage for role clarity and employee engagement. Clifford (1994) defines job analysis as "the process of defining the work, activities, tasks, products, services, or processes performed by or produced by an employee" (p. 321). A thorough job analysis provides nonprofit leaders with several important pieces of information about the jobs within their organization, including job descriptions and job specifications. A *job description* refers to the tasks, duties, and responsibilities that employees will be required to perform. *Job specifications* describe the person-based knowledge, skills, abilities, and other characteristics a prospective employee likely needs to possess in order to perform a job well. When nonprofit leaders articulate up front what new hires will actually be responsible for doing and the behavioral and performance standards they will need to achieve, as well as accurately identify what combination of know-how and prior experience appropriately enables applicants to be hired in the first place and best prepares them for success, they are planting the seeds of worker confidence and workforce engagement.

Two other HR tools that enable role clarity and worker successes are onboarding and orientation programs and new-hire training. Cable et al. (2013) note that well done onboarding processes "can help new hires become more connected with their colleagues, more engaged in their work and more likely to stay" (p. 23). High-quality orientation programs help acclimate individuals to the employer and their coworkers and leaders and facilitate an understanding about their role in and potential contributions to the organization. Beyond the more general nature of onboarding and orientation efforts, new-hire training programs are designed to specifically ensure that employee specifications (i.e., knowledge, skills, and abilities) become aligned with the tasks, duties, and responsibilities of their new job. Regardless of a new-hire's prior experience or level of competency, there is always a transition process when joining a new organization or taking on a new role. There are new internal procedures to learn, different technologies to get used to, new people to get accustomed to working with, and so on. A strong initial training program can help workers settle into new roles, gain clarity about what is expected of them, and grow in their confidence and performance capabilities.

Continuous and effective performance management is another HR lever than can help drive employee role clarity, motivation, and engagement and positive outcomes. Deanne den Hartog et al. (2004) describe performance management as a multifaceted process that involves "defining, measuring, and stimulating employee performance with the ultimate goal of improving organizational performance" (p. 556). Gruman and Saks (2011) argue that a more appropriate term than performance management might be "performance facilitation" given the increasingly complex nature of jobs and job performance, as well as the fact that today's managers are as much involved creating wide-reaching organizational conditions that enable performance as they are managing individual employee attitudes and behaviors. As described earlier, an important element of role clarity is communication concerning one's performance and whether or not they are meeting behavioral and achievement expectations. A regular and transparent performance management or facilitation process can help create regular flows of information and job feedback. Many organizations conduct annual performance reviews (if at all), but biannual or even more frequent reviews are becoming increasingly popular. In the case of employee performance that meets or exceeds expectations, such information can reinforce an employee's work efforts and motivate them to continue contributing in valuable ways. Where one's performance might be deficient, timely and honest feedback can help workers better understand where their efforts are misaligned with departmental or organizational objectives and how they can improve. Either way, high-quality performance facilitation is a job resource that can spark energy, motivation, and employee engagement.

Supervisor and Coworker Support

Social support from individuals at work—especially from one's supervisor and coworkers—has been shown to be an important driver of positive employment outcomes. High levels of supervisor and coworker support lead to fewer workplace errors and greater service recovery and helping behaviors (Pasamehmetoglu et al., 2017), enhance workers' ability to exert emotional labor during service work (Kim et al., 2017), and increase safety compliance and participation (Guo et al., 2019). Support from supervisors, coworkers, or both also enables workers to better cope with workloads and workplace tensions (Kirmeyer & Dougherty, 1988), encourages more knowledge sharing within organizations (Chae et al., 2019), and even spurs innovation behaviors among workers (Yang et al., 2020). Taken together, social support by way of supervisor and coworker support functions as an important job resource that heightens employee confidence, motivates workers to perform at their best and yields an engaged workforce.

How nonprofit leaders might leverage HR practices in order to foster strong social support systems is perhaps less obvious than many of the managerial interventions we have discussed up to this point. Sometimes, human resource management is relatively straightforward—do X and Y will happen (at least in theory). At other times, the line of sight between leadership activities and employee engagement is not a line at all, but instead a series of interactions and relationships between individual and organizational dynamics. Similar to the concept of performance facilitation described above, the creation of strong supervisor and coworker support systems likely involves nonprofit managers becoming skilled at creating complex organizational conditions which enable the development of a climate of social support (as opposed to directly managing individual attitudes and behaviors). One way to leverage human resources to facilitate social support, then, is to enact and promote practices that tap into supervisors' and coworkers' abilities, motivation, and opportunities to engage in supportive behaviors. The ability–motivation–opportunity (AMO) model of human resource management provides a framework for how this can happen.

As described by Jiang et al. (2012), the AMO model of HR posits that organizational systems can induce desired outcomes by promoting and enacting management practices that develop workers' skills around doing desired behaviors (ability), providing desired incentives that appropriately motivate such behavior (motivation), and creating opportunities for people to engage in wanted organizational activities (opportunity). Practically applied to supervisor and coworker support, this means devising HR practices that: (1) ensure supervisors and coworkers are capable of providing the organization's employees with high-quality and meaningful support, (2) give supervisors and coworkers a reason for wanting to be supportive of others in the first place, and (3) afford supervisors and coworkers instances where they can actually support organizational members. An example of an ability-focused HR practice would be providing education and training to supervisors on effective communications and relationship management. An example of a motivation-focused HR practice would be including collaboration and teamwork as metrics that are regularly evaluated as part of the performance management or facilitation process. As the adage goes, "what gets measured gets done." And an example of an opportunity-focused HR practice would include scheduling routine department or organization-wide gatherings that enabled information sharing or allowed employees to celebrate performance accomplishments or work milestones.

Organizational Fairness Perceptions and Trust in Senior Leadership

An engaged workforce depends on employees feeling as though they are treated fairly in the workplace. Equally important is that workers trust in the decision-making capabilities and actions of senior organization leaders. In management scholarship, the concept of employer-focused fairness is often couched as organizational justice, and two important types of organizational justice are distributive justice and procedural justice.

Distributive justice has to do with how equitably outcomes (such as pay or annual raises) are distributed among employees, whereas procedural justice considers the extent to which organizational processes used to determine the allocation of outcomes (such as performance appraisals) are free from bias and applied consistently (Colquitt et al., 2005). When workers have high organizational justice perceptions of their employers, they work harder to meet job responsibilities and attain organizational goals (Folger & Konovsky, 1989; Kim & Mauborgne, 1991), experience positive feelings at work (Colquitt et al., 2013), feel closer ties (Tyler & Blader, 2003), and identify more strongly (Olkkonen & Lipponen, 2006) with the organization. Outcomes like these and others are precursors to employee engagement and a high-performing organization.

Perceptions of a fair and equitable workplace do not materialize merely as a result of the behaviors of supervisors or even HR department personnel. Equally influential are the overarching organizational strategies and governance structures that influence line and staff leader decisions about resource allocation processes and outcomes and that ultimately impact workers. As Haynie et al. (2016) write, "senior managers are the paramount authority responsible for...strategic direction and oversight of internal governance structures." "As such," they continue, "trust that employees develop in senior managers...is partly shaped by experiences [they] have with various organizational systems as well as their broader perceptions about the effectiveness with which senior managers have guided the organization" (p. 890). Macey and Schneider (2008) found that in order for employees to become fully engaged at work, they must trust those senior leaders charged with enacting fair and just outcomes and procedures in the first place. All this suggests a complex, interactive, and necessary relationship between organizational justice perceptions, trust in senior leadership, and employee engagement.

What, then, can nonprofit organizations do to enhance perceptions of distributive and procedural justice and build their workforce's trust in senior leadership? One approach is to strive for organizational policies and procedures, especially around hiring and compensation, that employees perceive to be legitimate and fair. Equity theory (Adams, 1963) suggests that employees are not only concerned with the absolute realities of allocated outcomes (such as how much annual salary they make), but also with how distributions compare to their own level of effort and the level of effort of others. As such, nonprofit leaders should place equity concerns front and center when designing HR policies and deciding how resources will be provided to workers. Importantly, this does not mean that outcomes must be exactly the same for each and every employee. Human resource management scholars have described an organizational approach to talent management termed "segmentation" or "differentiation" whereby varying levels of investments are made in specific jobs and specific people when those jobs and people are intended to create disproportionately high value for the organization and uniquely contribute to its strategic success. Such an approach might actually lead to lower overall personnel expenses since employees are not unnecessarily overpaid paid across the organization (Becker and Huselid, 1998; Lepak & Snell, 1999). The key when implementing any HR policy, differentiated or otherwise, is to ensure that the reasons behind resource allocations are made without bias and favoritism and that both the processes and the outcomes are clearly explained to employees.

Relatedly, constant and meaningful communication from nonprofit executives is a must when it comes to employee trust and confidence in senior organization leaders. Organization managers can enhance employee engagement by enacting robust governance systems (Mayer & Davis, 1999) and collaborative management practices (Mossholder et al., 2011), frequently providing timely and rich information to employees (Ellis & Shockley-Zalabak, 2001), and becoming transformational leaders who consult with employees and involve them in decision-making (Burke et al., 2007). The creation of an organizational climate of care and concern, as was described above during the discussion of work–life balance, is also influential in building trust between employees and senior leaders and can serve as a conduit between fairness perceptions and workforce engagement.

Table 4.1 lays out each of these job resources, why and how they matter for employee engagement, and the human resource practices leaders can utilize to enhance their presence within nonprofit organizations.

Conclusion

At just about every turn, managers and leaders are hearing or talking about employee engagement. There is a good explanation for this—a disengaged employee can cost an employer up to 18% of that worker's annual salary in lost productivity (Herway, 2020). Such a lack of

Table 4.1 Enhancing employee engagement through human resource management and the creation of job resources

Job resource	How it affects employees and relates to workforce engagement	HR practices that nonprofit organizations and leaders can leverage to drive employee engagement
Work-life balance	• A healthy balance between an employee's work and non-work responsibilities is beneficial for their own health and well-being, and that of their families • Quality of work-life is correlated with lower employee stress, anxiety, and depression • Employee balance is related to greater job satisfaction, organizational commitment, and job performance • When people feel a sense of balance, they are less likely to quit	• On-site, emergency, and seasonal childcare programs • Eldercare initiatives such as referral programs and case management • Robust parental and family leave policies • External and on-site educational and training opportunities • Generous vacation and leave policies such as sabbaticals, community service leaves, educational leaves, and other organization- or self-funded breaks that allow for self-development and rest
Employee health and wellness	• Healthy employees have higher work performance and report a higher overall quality of life • Employees who participate in employer-sponsored health promotion programs have higher job satisfaction and lower absenteeism and turnover rates • Healthy employees incur fewer workplace injuries and lower workers' compensation costs	• Offering wellness events, services, and other resources as part of an employer-initiated health promotion program • Ensuring an effective health and wellness strategy through careful assessment, leadership buy-in, ground-up employee support, targeted program goals and objectives, adequate investments of financial resources, organization-wide communication, and program measurement

Job resource	How it affects employees and relates to workforce engagement	HR practices that nonprofit organizations and leaders can leverage to drive employee engagement
Flexible work arrangements	• Increased workplace flexibility is positively related to productivity, job performance, and employee engagement • Shifting from a time-focused working environment to one that is focused more on employee results can reduce turnover by more than 45%	• Switching away from a time-focused, effort-oriented culture of "clocking in" that is overly concerned with meeting standard time and place prescriptions to one that honors performance and results • Remote or hybrid work • Flextime or flexible working time agreements • Compressed work weeks (such as four 10-hour days instead of five 8-hour days) • Basing work efforts and hours around job tasks and deliverables rather than duration minimums • Job sharing
Role clarity	• Having a clear understanding of one's role and what is expected at work enables employees to become more confident in their performance capabilities • The lack of role clarity leads to workers becoming frustrated with the work environment and burned out	• Purposefully specifying the task, duties, and responsibilities (i.e., job description) needed to perform a job well when envisioning and creating jobs. For existing jobs, conduct a thorough job analysis to ensure that job descriptions accurately capture expectations for employee contributions • Be clear about the job specifications (i.e., knowledge, skills, abilities, experience, and other competencies) employees must possess in order to perform a job well • Write clear position descriptions that reflect carefully crafted job descriptions and job specifications • Conduct onboarding and orientation programs and new-hire training • Make high-quality performance management and facilitation a routine practice within the organization

(continued)

Table 4.1 (continued)

Job resource	How it affects employees and relates to workforce engagement	HR practices that nonprofit organizations and leaders can leverage to drive employee engagement
Supervisor and coworker social support	• Social support for individuals at work, especially from one's supervisor and coworkers, leads to fewer workplace errors and increases safety compliance • Employees exhibit more workplace-helping behaviors when social support is high • Greater support levels result in more effective service recovery and emotional labor during service-oriented tasks • Knowledge sharing and innovation behaviors are enhanced in workplaces with high social support from supervisors and coworkers	• Create and promote an organizational climate of social support and helping behaviors in the workplace • Train and otherwise ensure that supervisors and coworkers know how to be supportive to organization members • Model desired support behaviors and use rewards to incentivize social support • Create opportunities for social support, information sharing, and network and friendship formation to occur (e.g., department gatherings or organization wide celebrations)
Employee fairness perceptions and trust in senior leadership	• When workers perceive their work environments to be fair, they work harder to meet job responsibilities and attain organizational goals • Employees experience greater positive feelings at work and feel closer ties with and identify more strongly with their organizations when justice perceptions are high • Because employees often view senior leaders as ultimately responsible for the establishment of fair (or unfair) organizational policies and practices, trust in senior leadership is a precursor to perceptions of distributive and procedural justice and, ultimately, engagement	• Ensure that organizational policies and procedures, especially around hiring, compensation, and the allocation of rewards and tangible outcomes, are legitimate, fair, and free from bias • Periodically audit HR practices to ensure high degrees of fairness • Regularly communicate organizational policies and any changes in procedures, and provide employees with timely and detail-rich information • Involve employees in organizational decision-making • Encourage transformational leadership behaviors from senior leaders

performance potential adds up to a lot of missed opportunities to sufficiently meet client needs and effectively serve communities. But job and organizational resources such as work–life balance, employee health and wellness, flexible work arrangements, role clarity, supervisor and coworker social support, and employee perceptions of organizational fairness and their level of trust in senior organization leadership can counter motivation-sapping job demands, spark employee energy and commitment, and maximize job engagement and organizational performance. Innovative, employee-centered human resource practices hold great promise for nonprofit leaders looking to create and sustain an engaged workforce.

REFERENCES

Akingbola, K., & Van Den Berg, H. A. (2019). Antecedents, consequences, and context of employee engagement in nonprofit organizations. *Review of Public Personnel Administration, 39*(1), 46–74.

Allen, T. D., Herst, D. E. L., Bruck, C. S., & Sutton, M. (2000). Consequences associated with work-to-family conflict: A review and agenda for future research. *Journal of Occupational Health Psychology, 5*, 278–308.

Bal, P. M., & De Lange, A. H. (2015). From flexibility human resource management to employee engagement and perceived job performance across the lifespan: A multisample study. *Journal of Occupational and Organizational Psychology, 88*(1), 126–154.

Becker, B. E., & Huselid, M. A. (1998). High performance work systems and firm performance: A synthesis of research and managerial implications. In *Research in personnel and human resource management*.

Berger, L. A., & Berger, D. R. (2004). *The talent management handbook*. McGraw-Hill.

Adams, J. S. (1963). Towards an understanding of inequity. *The Journal of Abnormal and Social Psychology, 67*(5), 422.

Bernacki, E. J., & Baun, W. B. (1984). The relationship of job performance to exercise adherence in a corporate fitness program. *Journal of Occupational Medicine*, 529–531.

Breslow, L., Fielding, J., Herrman, A. A., & Wilbur, C. S. (1990). Worksite health promotion: Its evolution and the Johnson & Johnson experience. *Preventive Medicine, 19*(1), 13–21.

Burke, C. S., Sims, D. E., Lazzara, E. H., & Salas, E. (2007). Trust in leadership: A multi-level review and integration. *The Leadership Quarterly, 18*(6), 606–632.

Cable, D. M., Gino, F., & Staats, B. R. (2013). Reinventing employee onboarding. *MIT Sloan Management Review, 54*(3), 23.

Canadian Centre for Occupational Health and Safety. *OSH answers fact sheet.* https://www.ccohs.ca/oshanswers/psychosocial/worklife_balance.html#:~: text=What%20are%20work%2Flife%20balance,enjoyment)%20of%20life%20o utside%20work. Accessed June 14, 2022.

Centers for Disease Control and Prevention. *Engaging employees in their health and wellness.* https://www.cdc.gov/workplacehealthpromotion/initia tives/resource-center/case-studies/engage-employees-health-wellness.html. Accessed June 14, 2022.

Chae, H., Park, J., & Choi, J. N. (2019). Two facets of conscientiousness and the knowledge sharing dilemmas in the workplace: Contrasting moderating functions of supervisor support and coworker support. *Journal of Organizational Behavior, 40*(4), 387–399.

Clifford, J. P. (1994). Job analysis: Why do it, and how should it be done? *Public Personnel Management, 23*(2), 321–340.

Colquitt, J. A., Greenberg, J., & Zapata-Phelan, C. P. (2005). What is organizational justice? A historical overview. In J. Greenberg & J. A. Colquitt (Eds.), *Handbook of Organizational Justice* (pp. 3–56). Erlbaum.

Colquitt, J. A., Scott, B. A., Rodell, J. B., Long, D. M., Zapata, C. P., Conlon, D. E., & Wesson, M. J. (2013). Justice at the millennium, a decade later: A meta-analytic test of social exchange and affect-based perspectives. *Journal of Applied Psychology, 98*(2), 199.

Culture Amp. *Non profits United States 2022.* https://www.cultureamp.com/sci ence/insights/nonprofit-united-states. Accessed June 3, 2022.

Demerouti, E., Bakker, A. B., Nachreiner, F., & Schaufeli, W. B. (2001). The job demands-resources model of burnout. *Journal of Applied Psychology, 86*(3), 499.

Den Hartog, D. N., Boselie, P., & Paauwe, J. (2004). Performance management: A model and research agenda. *Applied Psychology: An International Review, 53*(4), 556–569.

Eby, L. T., Casper, W. J., Lockwood, A., Bordeaux, C., & Brinley, A. (2005). Work and family research in IO/OB: Content analysis and review of the literature (1980–2002). *Journal of Vocational Behavior, 66*(1), 124–197.

Ellis, K., & Shockley-Zalabak, P. (2001). Trust in top management and immediate supervisor: The relationship to satisfaction, perceived organizational effectiveness, and information receiving. *Communication Quarterly, 49*(4), 382–398.

Folger, R., & Konovsky, M. A. (1989). Effects of procedural and distributive justice on reactions to pay raise decisions. *Academy of Management Journal, 32*(1), 115–130.

Frögéli, E., Rudman, A., & Gustavsson, P. (2019). The relationship between task mastery, role clarity, social acceptance, and stress: An intensive longitudinal study with a sample of newly registered nurses. *International Journal of Nursing Studies, 91,* 60–69.

Gartner. (2022, June 16). *9 future of work trends post Covid-19.* https://www.gartner.com/smarterwithgartner/9-future-of-work-trends-post-covid-19. Accessed June 17, 2022.

Golaszewski, T., Snow, D., Lynch, W., Yen, L., & Solomita, D. (1992). A benefit-to-cost analysis of a work-site health promotion program. *Journal of Occupational Medicine,* 1164–1172.

Gruman, J. A., & Saks, A. M. (2011). Performance management and employee engagement. *Human Resource Management Review, 21*(2), 123–136.

Guo, M., Liu, S., Chu, F., Ye, L., & Zhang, Q. (2019). Supervisory and coworker support for safety: Buffers between job insecurity and safety performance of high-speed railway drivers in China. *Safety Science, 117,* 290–298.

Haar, J. M., Russo, M., Suñe, A., & Ollier-Malaterre, A. (2014). Outcomes of work–life balance on job satisfaction, life satisfaction and mental health: A study across seven cultures. *Journal of Vocational Behavior, 85*(3), 361–373.

Halbesleben, J. R. (2010). A meta-analysis of work engagement: Relationships with burnout, demands, resources, and consequences. In A. B. Bakker & M. P. Leiter (Eds.), *Work engagement: A handbook of essential theory and research* (pp. 102–117). Psychology Press.

Harter, J. (2022, March 18). *Percent who feel employer cares about their wellbeing plummets.* https://www.gallup.com/workplace/390776/percent-feel-employer-cares-wellbeing-plummets.aspx#:~:text=Fewer%20than%20one%20in%20four,percentage%20in%20nearly%20a%20decade

Harter, J. K., Schmidt, F. L., Agrawal, S., Plowman, S. K., & Blue, A. (2020a). The relationship between engagement at work and organizational outcomes. *2020 Q12 Meta-Analysis: Gallup* (10th ed.). https://www.mandalidis.ch/coaching/2021/01/2020-employee-engagement-meta-analysis.pdf

Harter, J. K., Schmidt, F. L., Agrawal, S., Blue, A., Plowman, S. K., Josh, P., & Asplund, J. (2020b). *The relationship between engagement at work and organizational outcomes.* https://www.gallup.com/workplace/321725/gallup-q12-meta-analysis-report.aspx. Accessed June 14, 2022.

Harvard Business Review Analytic Services. (2013). *The impact of employee engagement on performance.* https://hbr.org/resources/pdfs/comm/achievers/hbr_achievers_report_sep13.pdf. Accessed June 14, 2022.

Haynie, J. J., Mossholder, K. W., & Harris, S. G. (2016). Justice and job engagement: The role of senior management trust. *Journal of Organizational Behavior, 37*(6), 889–910.

Herway, J. (2020, October 15). *Increase productivity at the lowest possible cost*. https://www.gallup.com/workplace/321743/increase-productivity-lowest-possible-cost.aspx. Accessed August 20, 2022.

Institute for Health and Productivity Studies, Johns Hopkins Bloomberg School of Public Health. *From evidence to practice: Workplace wellness that works, 2015*. https://www.transamericacenterforhealthstudies.org/docs/default-source/wellness-page/from-evidence-to-practice—workplace-wellness-that-works.pdf?sfvrsn=2. Accessed June 14, 2022.

Jiang, K., Lepak, D. P., Hu, J., & Baer, J. C. (2012). How does human resource management influence organizational outcomes? A meta-analytic investigation of mediating mechanisms. *Academy of Management Journal, 55*(6), 1264–1294.

Johansen, M. S., & Sowa, J. E. (2019). Human resource management, employee engagement, and nonprofit hospital performance. *Nonprofit Management and Leadership, 29*(4), 549–567.

Kahn, W. A. (1990). Psychological conditions of personal engagement and disengagement at work. *Academy of Management Journal, 33*, 692–724.

Kim, H. J., Hur, W. M., Moon, T. W., & Jun, J. K. (2017). Is all support equal? The moderating effects of supervisor, coworker, and organizational support on the link between emotional labor and job performance. *Business Research Quarterly, 20*(2), 124–136.

Kim, W. C., & Mauborgne, R. A. (1991). Implementing global strategies: The role of procedural justice. *Strategic Management Journal, 12*(S1), 125–143.

Kirmeyer, S. L., & Dougherty, T. W. (1988). Work load, tension, and coping: Moderating effects of supervisor support. *Personnel Psychology, 41*(1), 125–139.

Lepak, D. P., & Snell, S. A. (1999). The human resource architecture: Toward a theory of human capital allocation and development. *Academy of Management Review, 24*(1), 31–48.

Macey, W. H., & Schneider, B. (2008). Engaged in engagement: We are delighted we did it. *Industrial and Organizational Psychology, 1*(1), 76–83.

Mayer, R. C., & Davis, J. H. (1999). The effect of the performance appraisal system on trust for management: A field quasi-experiment. *Journal of Applied Psychology, 84*(1), 123.

McKinsey & Company. (2022, June 23). *Americans are embracing flexible work—And they want more of it*. https://www.mckinsey.com/industries/real-estate/our-insights/americans-are-embracing-flexible-work-and-they-want-more-of-it. Accessed June 17, 2022.

Moen, P., Kelly, E. L., & Hill, R. (2011). Does enhancing work-time control and flexibility reduce turnover? *A Naturally Occurring Experiment. Social Problems, 58*(1), 69–98.

Mossholder, K. W., Richardson, H. A., & Settoon, R. P. (2011). Human resource systems and helping in organizations: A relational perspective. *Academy of Management Review, 36*(1), 33–52.

Olkkonen, M. E., & Lipponen, J. (2006). Relationships between organizational justice, identification with organization and work unit, and group-related outcomes. *Organizational Behavior and Human Decision Processes, 100*(2), 202–215.

Parkes, L. P., & Langford, P. H. (2008). Work–life balance or work–life alignment? A test of the importance of work-life balance for employee engagement and intention to stay in organisations. *Journal of Management & Organization, 14*(3), 267–284.

Pasamehmetoglu, A., Guchait, P., Tracey, J. B., Cunningham, C. J., & Lei, P. (2017). The moderating effect of supervisor and coworker support for error management on service recovery performance and helping behaviors. *Journal of Service Theory and Practice, 27*(1), 2–22.

Pocock, B. (2003). *The work/life collision: What work is doing to Australians and what to do about it.* Federation Press.

Rich, B. L., Lepine, J. A., & Crawford, E. R. (2010). Job engagement: Antecedents and effects on job performance. *Academy of Management Journal, 53*(3), 617–635.

Saks, A. M. (2022). Caring human resources management and employee engagement. *Human Resource Management Review, 32*(3).

Saks, A. M., & Gruman, J. A. (2014). What do we really know about employee engagement? *Human Resource Development Quarterly, 25*(2), 155–182.

Schaufeli, W. B. (2017). Applying the job demands-resources model. *Organizational Dynamics, 2*(46), 120–132.

Schaufeli, W. B., Salanova, M., González-Romá, V., & Bakker, A. B. (2002). The measurement of engagement and burnout: A two sample confirmatory factor analytic approach. *Journal of Happiness Studies, 3*(1), 71–92.

Shephard, R. J. (1992). Twelve years experience of a fitness program for the salaried employees of a Toronto life assurance company. *American Journal of Health Promotion, 6*(4), 292–301.

Tyler, T. R., & Blader, S. L. (2003). The group engagement model: Procedural justice, social identity, and cooperative behavior. *Personality and Social Psychology Review, 7*(4), 349–361.

Wayne, J. H., Musisca, N., & Fleeson, W. (2004). Considering the role of personality in the work–family experience: Relationships of the big five to work–family conflict and facilitation. *Journal of Vocational Behavior, 64*(1), 108–130.

Zheng, X., Thundiyil, T., Klinger, R., & Hinrichs, A. T. (2016). Curvilinear relationships between role clarity and supervisor satisfaction. *Journal of Managerial Psychology, 31*(1), 110–126.

Yang, W., Hao, Q., & Song, H. (2020). Linking supervisor support to innovation implementation behavior via commitment: the moderating role of coworker support. *Journal of Managerial Psychology*.

WTW. (2019, May 7). *The power of three: Taking engagement to new heights.* https://www.wtwco.com/en-US/Insights/2016/02/the-power-of-three-taking-engagement-to-new-heights#:~:text=Engaged%20employees%20outperform%20their%20non,now%20widely%20accepted%20as%20fact. Accessed August 19, 2022.

WTW. (2021, May). *Why is employee engagement important?* https://www.wtwco.com/en-US/Insights/2021/05/why-is-employee-engagement-important. Accessed August 20, 2022.

CHAPTER 5

Volunteer Engagement

Volunteers are vital resources for nonprofit organizations. They help organizations quickly acquire relevant experience, deep knowledge, and value-adding skills. In many cases, volunteers help extend a nonprofit's reach into a wider range of locations and populations, and in other cases, volunteers provide the direct services that enable agencies to keep their doors open and deliver vital programs to people and communities in need. Volunteers often provide advanced managerial capabilities to nonprofits, with motivated individuals enthusiastically serving as board members and fundraisers or overseeing special events or projects. Importantly, volunteers empower nonprofits to meet the needs of individual and organizational clients, local communities, and a global society more effectively.

Understanding volunteer engagement and how to foster it is a key ingredient in nonprofit organizational success. This chapter examines the role, process, and challenges of engaging volunteers within nonprofit organizations. After setting the stage for volunteer engagement by considering the reasons why volunteers volunteer in the first place, we discuss several ways that nonprofits can leverage administrative and people-centered management practices to develop and foster an engaged volunteer force. To be sure, much of what was discussed in Chapter 4 about employee engagement generally applies to volunteers. However, given the uniqueness of volunteers and their contributions to nonprofit organizations, a specific treatment of volunteers and volunteer engagement is warranted. The goal of this chapter is to equip nonprofit leaders, volunteer administrators, and students aspiring to become change agents in nonprofits with research-backed practical advice for enhancing volunteer engagement within organizations.

VOLUNTEER MOTIVES AS A BASIS FOR ENGAGEMENT

Several academic disciplines have explored why people donate their time, talent, and energy in support of community interests and societal causes. Psychologists have examined the various needs people seek to fulfill through their volunteerism, while sociologists have considered whether certain personal or environmental determinants are more likely to be associated with donating one's labor. Even economists and political scientists, as well as scholars from several other fields of study, have contributed to our understanding of volunteering.

Grasping the potential drivers of volunteer participation is a necessary first step in our examination of volunteer engagement. But why? Because creating and enhancing organizational engagement is all about tapping into and feeding those things which are important to members of a nonprofit workforce. A deeper understanding of the reasons why people volunteer forms a strong basis from which managers and leaders can promote positive workplace engagement.

Psychological Explanations for Volunteerism

Much attention has been given to the psychological underpinnings of volunteerism. According to the American Psychological Association, psychology is the study of the human mind and behavior. The APA further describes psychology as the "collection of behaviors, traits, attitudes, and so forth that characterize an individual or a group." When it comes to explaining why people volunteer, psychology scholars are often focused on what people are thinking about themselves and about others, an individual's personality, and what individuals or groups of individuals perceive their needs to be, among other considerations.

A popular way of thinking about volunteer motives from a psychological perspective comes from the Volunteer Functional Inventory or VFI (Clary et al., 1998). The VFI takes a functionalist, needs-based approach to understand donative behavior and posits that people freely give their time and talent to nonprofits and other organizations because doing so fulfills some partially unmet psychological need (Musick & Wilson, 2007; Snyder et al., 2000). It focuses on six psychological needs in particular—personal understanding and growth, psychological protection, career development, social fulfillment, learning and experience enhancement, and value actualization. Volunteering becomes a vehicle for individuals and groups to participate in experiences that help meet these psychological needs. Table 5.1 describes these six functions and provides examples of each.

Fulfilling needs is not the only way psychologists explore volunteer motivation. Attributes such as one's personality or attitudes also influence donative behavior. Volunteer participation is higher among individuals who rate highly on such personality traits as self-efficacy (a person's belief in their own capabilities), empathy, emotional stability, and morality (Allen & Rushton, 1983). Additionally, people are more likely to volunteer when they view a cause or organization's purpose as interesting, satisfying, attractive, meaningful, and important (Chacko, 1985; Cook, 1984; Hodgkinson et al., 1992).

Sociological and Other Academic Explanations for Volunteerism

Whereas psychologists often focus on a person's thoughts or attitudes to explain volunteer participation, sociologists tend to examine how structural forces—such as a person's environment or their social background—influence the decision to volunteer. As the American Sociological Association notes, "[S]ociology is the study of social life, social change, and the social causes and consequences of human behavior. Sociologists investigate the structure of groups, organizations, and societies and how people interact within these contexts." The sociological study of volunteerism, thus, has focused on the role contextual and situational factors play in people deciding to donate their time and energy to nonprofit causes. Such factors include education levels, occupation, marital status, gender, parental status, neighborhood location, and the like.

For example, having higher levels of education, a job high in occupational prestige, high family income and wealth, and school-aged children living at home are associated with greater volunteer participation rates (Lemon et al., 1972; Smith, 1994). Additionally, higher volunteerism

Table 5.1 Needs-based reasons for why people volunteer according to the volunteer functional inventory

Personal Understanding and Growth	Volunteering serves as an ego-boosting activity that enhances one's self-esteem, self-image, and confidence in themselves. In surveys, some questions that are asked to measure this dimension might include "volunteering makes me feel needed," "volunteering makes me feel important," and "volunteering increases my self-esteem"
Psychological Protection	Volunteering enables people to deal with uncertainty, inner conflicts, and emotional needs. For example, someone dealing with a medical condition might volunteer for a foundation focused on curing that condition as a way to cope with their fears about disease or to become connected with others who have also been diagnosed. In surveys, some questions that are asked to measure this dimension might include "no matter how bad I have been feeling, volunteering helps me to forget about it," "volunteering helps me work through my own problems," and "by volunteering I feel less lonely"
Career Development	Volunteering helps develop one's work-related knowledge and skills and builds career personal networks. In surveys, some questions that are asked to measure this dimension might include "volunteering can help me get my foot in the door at a place where I would like to work," "volunteering allows me to explore different career options," "I can make new contacts that can help my career," and "volunteering experience looks good on my resume"

Social Fulfillment	People volunteer in order to socially interact with individuals and groups that are meaningful to them. In surveys, some questions that are asked to measure this dimension might include "my friends volunteer," "people I am close with want me to volunteer," "people I know share an interest in community service," and "volunteering is an important activity to the people I know best"
Learning and Experience Enhancement	Volunteering enables people to gain and sustain personal abilities and competencies. It can also allow them to expand their perspective on causes and issues. In surveys, some questions that are asked to measure this dimension might include "volunteering allows me to gain a new perspective on things," "I can learn how to deal with a variety of people by volunteering," "volunteering lets me learn new things through direct, hands-on experiences"
Value Actualization	Through volunteering, people can express altruism and engage in activities that support a desired or ideal conception of themselves. In surveys, some questions that are asked to measure this dimension might include "I am concerned about those less fortunate than myself," "I feel compassion toward people in need," "I can do something for a cause that is important to me," and "I am genuinely concerned about the particular group I am serving"

rates have been found among individuals living in wealthier neighborhoods as well as rural communities (Bell & Force, 1956; Curtis et al., 1992). Gender as a determinant of volunteerism yields inconclusive results, with some studies finding that women volunteer more (e.g., Hodgkinson & Weitzman, 1986; Hodgkinson et al., 1992), others finding that men volunteer more (e.g., Curtis et al., 1992; Palisi & Korn, 1989), and still others not finding any gender differences in volunteer participation rates (e.g., Auslander & Litwin, 1988; Berger, 1991). Across many studies that examine the relationship between gender and volunteerism, type of activity and organization (e.g., church, sports coaching and recreation, charities, school, or neighborhood activities, etc.) appears to play some role. In terms of race, two studies found that nonwhites, and Blacks, in particular, have higher rates of social and political volunteerism (Bobo & Gilliam, 1990; Florin et al., 1986). More generally, however, being white and middle-aged is associated with higher levels of volunteer activity (Smith, 1994).

Other academic disciplines, such as economics and political science, have also contributed to our understanding of why people volunteer. In what might be the simplest and most obvious explanation, Harvard Economist Richard Freeman found that being asked by another person to volunteer is a primary predictor of one's decision to volunteer, especially if that person is a friend or someone close to you (Freeman, 1997). Relatedly, already having close ties with people who volunteer for an organization or specific cause also spurs people to volunteer more, and people who espouse such values as patriotism, concern for national issues and progress, and political democracy tend to volunteer at higher rates (Hougland & Christenson, 1982).

CREATING EFFECTIVE VOLUNTEER ENGAGEMENT

Equipped with a solid understanding of why volunteers give their time, talent, and energy to agencies and organizations, nonprofit leaders can create effective engagement strategies and practices that tap into volunteer motives, deepen volunteer commitment to nonprofits and the clients they serve, and maximize volunteer performance and service contributions. The remainder of this chapter outlines several areas where nonprofits can leverage leadership skills to harness the benefits of volunteer engagement and create a high-performing organization—value alignment; enhanced work design; continuous development, performance management, and organizational learning; constructive volunteer-employee relations; and recognition and rewards. The discussion that follows speaks to tangible steps nonprofit managers can take to create an engaged volunteer workforce. Measuring engagement, such as through climate surveys, is discussed later in Chapter 9.

Value Alignment

Values are deep-seated dispositions that drive individual behavior, including people's contributions in the workplace. As previously discussed, value actualization is an important motivator among volunteers, since they seek to participate in activities that allow them to live out their best and ideal self-conceptions. Leveraging commonalities between volunteer and organizational values becomes an important tool nonprofit managers and leaders can use to enhance volunteer commitment, loyalty, performance, and engagement.

Research suggests a strong link between the alignment of individual and organizational purpose and positive outcomes for both workers and organizations. High alignment between workforce and organizational values leads to more effective organizational responses to crises, greater organizational performance, stronger organization-level competitive advantage, and enhanced employee commitment (Dearlove & Coomber, 1999). Those who perceive a high degree of personal and organizational alignment have greater feeling that they are successful and making a difference at work, have higher self-confidence, behave more ethically and with greater integrity in the workplace, are more loyal to the organization, and have lower feelings of stress (Posner et al., 1985).

According to a 2022 study conduct by Qualtrics, a U.S.-based survey management software firm, workforce members who perceive their organization's mission, vision, and values to align with their own personal values are more likely to stay and not quit, recommend the organization to others as a great place to work and feel as though the contributions they make at work gives them a sense of personal accomplishment. Given how costly volunteer turnover can be for nonprofits, maintaining an engaged volunteer force is as important as ever for organizational performance and effectiveness. Volunteer recruitment is also a key issue for nonprofits, and more than half of the respondents in their survey would not even consider working at an organization if there were a mismatch in values. Thus, attracting prospective volunteers whose personal values align with those of the organization should be a primary goal for nonprofit human resource staff and organization leaders.

Generationally, the Qualtrics study found that value alignment at work mattered most for "Generation Z" and "Millennial" workers. According to the Pew Research Center, "Gen Z" describes people born between 1997 and 2012. This would represent volunteers who are up to age 25 in the year 2022. Millennials were born between 1981 and 1996 and would represent volunteers between ages 26 and 41 in the year 2022. Gen Z and Millennials, more so than Baby Boomers (those born between 1946 and 1964 and who are ages 58–76 in the year 2022), are more willing to leave an organization due to a lack of value alignment or choose not to work there in the first place. Younger generations also appear to be more sensitive not only to the alignment between their and their organization's core values but also to the values of individual and organizational partners and suppliers an organization does business with. Fifty-one percent of Gen Z respondents in the survey indicated a willingness to leave an organization due to misalignment between their personal values and the organizational values of extended partners and suppliers, compared to only 26% of Baby Boomers. As the composition of the volunteer workforce increasingly shifts from Baby Boomers and Generation X-ers to Millennials and Gen Z-ers, the most successful nonprofit leaders will be keenly aware of how value alignment impacts volunteer engagement.

Enhanced Work Design

The quality with which volunteer positions are designed and how people experience nonprofit organization environments while they are donating their time and effort has a tremendous impact on their attitudes, behaviors, and engagement. Quite a bit of research evidence exists demonstrating that volunteer roles are sometimes designed with less care and attention than are paid, employee positions. In a national study of nearly 3,000 U.S. nonprofits, Hager and Brudney (2004) discovered that less than half of the organizations in their sample maintained formal written position descriptions for volunteer roles. Only about a third of nonprofits in their sample conducted any sort of volunteer evaluation or performance management. The University of California at Irvine management professor Jone Pearce found that volunteer work tended to be less structured than the work of paid staff and that volunteers often have blurry organizational memberships and work responsibilities that are less formalized than employees (Pearce, 1993). She notes that this seems to be the result of volunteer contributions often being considered a peripheral activity within nonprofits, and says:

> Without differential labor costs [for volunteers] there is no need to develop precise job duties for compensation purposes. Since there are no labor markets to tie wages to, nor any need to protect internal equity in pay by justifying pay differences by variations in responsibilities, knowledge requirements, and so forth...there is no pressure to be precise about formal relationships. (p. 41)

Having subpar volunteer work design is a huge liability and missed opportunity for volunteer engagement and nonprofit performance, especially since so many nonprofits rely on volunteer participation in order to meet the needs of their clients and the communities they serve. Just how much volunteer performance and engagement might nonprofits be leaving "on the table" due to poor volunteer work design? How much more engaged might the volunteer workforce be if more and careful attention is paid to how their participation is channeled within nonprofit organizations? With proper planning, leaders can optimize volunteer work design and maximize volunteer engagement.

The Job Characteristics Model (Hackman et al., 1975), a classic theoretical framework in organization and management scholarship, provides nonprofit leaders with a roadmap for how to engage volunteers more fully in the work of agencies and community organizations. The premise of the Job Characteristics Model, or JCM, is rather simple—core aspects of work, such as the variety of skills a person utilizes or the amount of autonomy they exercise while working, influence a person's psychological state (for example, whether their work is meaningful to them). And these psychological perceptions have an impact on personal and work outcomes such as satisfaction, performance, and turnover. Figure 5.1 presents a simplified depiction of the JCM and how it can affect volunteer engagement.

The five core work dimensions of the JCM include skill variety, task identity, task significance, autonomy, and feedback. Applied to the context of volunteers in a nonprofit organization, skill variety refers to whether a volunteer performs tasks that are challenging and fully utilize their knowledge, skills, and capabilities. Task identity speaks to the degree

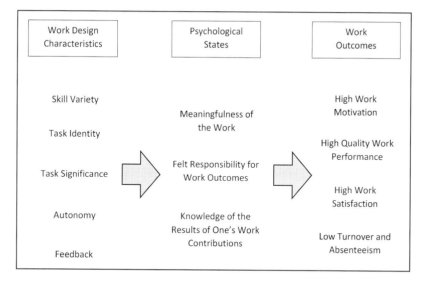

Fig. 5.1 A simplified depiction of the Hackman et al. Job characteristics theory

to which a volunteer's work contributes to a whole or identifiable end product. For example, if their only assignment is to sit in a cubicle and make phone calls as part of an annual fundraising campaign, and they are never permitted to take part in different aspects of the campaign such as public fund drives or celebratory events, their work could be described as having low task identity because they never see or take part in the larger effort of generating support and monetary donations for the nonprofit. Similarly, task significance also focuses on outcomes. What is different about this dimension, however, is that task significance is concerned with the degree to which the volunteer's work has a substantive impact on people and society. Unlike the task identity example above, a volunteer making routine fundraising calls from a cubicle might indeed report high task significance if they clearly understand that the money raised as a result of their phone calls helps provide, for example, life-saving access to healthcare for vulnerable populations.

Autonomy and feedback are the fourth and fifth dimensions of the JCM. Autonomy in this context refers to the extent to which volunteers are given freedom and flexibility in carrying out their tasks, as well as how much responsibility volunteers experience while donating their capabilities and knowledge. A highly autonomous position gives volunteers some measure of independence and discretion, enabling them to exercise their own initiative rather than solely relying upon step-by-step instructions from a supervisor or written organizational playbook. Interestingly, most nonprofits leaders appear not to provide volunteers much autonomy or space to exercise initiative. Across the national survey of almost 3,000 nonprofits mentioned earlier, Hager and Brudney (2004) found that 97% of them maintained strict supervision over their volunteer workforce. Finally, feedback refers to the extent to which volunteers become aware of the results of their contributions. This dimension is concerned with performance effectiveness—are there ways for me to know whether I am doing high-quality work? The feedback dimension is most effective in generating desired outcomes like high work satisfaction and low turnover when feedback is immediate or quick and comes directly from the work itself.

According to the JCM, work that is high in skill variety, task identity, task significance, autonomy, and feedback leads people to become more excited about their work and committed to their organizations. This happens because individuals perceive their contributions to be meaningful and significant to themselves and others. These positive perceptions make them happy about the work they are doing, motivate them to do it even more and better, and cause them to feel more attached to the organization and dissuade them from leaving it. Hackman and colleagues (1975) describe individuals in this virtuous cycle as "really prospering in their jobs" and argue that their "work is likely to be a lot like play." For nonprofit organizations, creating volunteer roles that facilitate enjoyable and fulfilling experiences is absolutely critical. Leaders and managers should understand that volunteer satisfaction, motivation, and commitment begin even before the volunteer commences their first assignment—the design of volunteer positions will have a tremendous impact on volunteer engagement and organizational success.

Continuous Development, Performance Management, and Organizational Learning

In his 1990 book *The Fifth Discipline*, author Peter Senge defines a learning organization as one that prioritizes opportunities for workers to continuously acquire knowledge and skills that add to their individual capabilities and an organization's success. Not only that, but learning organizations also make time and space for workers to collaborate and share information and best practices, present innovative ideas, make real decisions about the way work is done (remember "autonomy" from the JCM?), and even raise doubts and experiment with new methods in the workplace. Employee learning, "upskilling," and continuous development are perceived to be key ingredients for organizational competitiveness by a majority of corporate CEOs (Palmer & Blake, 2018), and when it comes to engaging an increasingly younger workforce, consulting firm Robert Half found that more than 90% of Generation Z employees view professional development as a key factor when choosing whether to work for an organization.

As discussed earlier in the chapter, volunteerism provides opportunities for people to fulfill a wide range of needs and desires, including personal understanding and growth, career development, and learning and enhancement. When these and other needs become fulfilled, participating volunteers become engaged volunteers and a host of positive benefits follow—volunteers may spread awareness and positive reputation of their agency and the services it provides, recruit other highly capable individuals to join and volunteer, or contribute to the nonprofit in ways beyond volunteering (e.g., philanthropy). Here are several questions nonprofit leaders and managers can periodically ask themselves to ensure they are effectively leveraging continuous development, performance management, and organizational learning in ways that maximize volunteer engagement:

- When volunteers join our organization, do we inventory their personal skills, capabilities, and desires in an attempt to match those with specific volunteer roles and organizational needs?
- After volunteers join our organization, do we periodically assess their satisfaction with the volunteering experience and inquire about any new personal learning and development goals?
- Are volunteers provided "volunteer development plans" or VDPs, akin to a career development plan that organizations might provide for paid employees? VDPs can be useful not only for the individual volunteer (such as helping to accurately assess and align their interests with organizational opportunities, thereby enhancing engagement) but also for volunteer workforce planning. For example, volunteer development planning might reveal that a certain highly

skilled volunteer only intends to stay with the organization for the next 12 months. This knowledge would enable a volunteer director to devise a plan for recruiting and onboarding a replacement volunteer prior to the current volunteer's departure, rather than being surprised by the volunteer's leaving and then the nonprofit going without that technical capability for a month or two as it scrambles to find a new volunteer.

- Is there a mentoring program for volunteers? This could be leader-to-volunteer, employee-to-volunteer, volunteer-to-volunteer, or some other format.
- Do we have an organizational culture that encourages volunteers to share their ideas, and are there mechanisms for volunteer voices to be heard, appreciated, and truly integrated into organizational decision-making? Do volunteers feel safe to speak their minds and make recommendations?
- Do our leaders provide timely and meaningful feedback to volunteers about the quality and effectiveness of their volunteer contributions? When contributions do not meet desired expectations, are volunteers provided guidance on how to better perform their assigned tasks?
- Is there a clear understanding of the value-add and return on investment (ROI) the organization receives from volunteer contributions? Are these metrics communicated to volunteers so that they are aware of the positive impact and significance of their time and energy donations?
- Is there a budget for volunteer training and development? (Hint: there should be).
- Are volunteers able to attend conferences, take online or local training courses, or otherwise access learning materials or opportunities that enhance their volunteer effectiveness (and subsequently, their engagement and the nonprofit's performance)?

Constructive Volunteer-Employee Relations

Positive workplace relations are crucial for any organization's success. Coworkers must be willing to seamlessly work alongside, share information with, and support one another if their organization is to effectively create products or service clients. Sadly, a 2010 Gallup study found that only 5% of workers strongly agree that their organization helps them develop positive interpersonal relationships at work. The same study reports that having a best friend at work increases one's engagement seven-fold, whereas those who are not socially embedded in their workplace only have an 8% chance of being engaged at work. Clearly, the quality of a workplace's social environment and the presence of constructive interpersonal relations have major implications for volunteer engagement.

Nonprofit leaders are especially at risk for leaving some volunteer engagement "on the table" when it comes to interpersonal relationship quality, given the unique organizational environment that results from mixing volunteer and paid workers. Social identity theory and self-categorization theory speak to complex group dynamics that occur based on personal identities and characteristics (Tajfel & Turner, 2004; Turner, 1987). People draw a sense of belonging and self-esteem by reflecting upon and being proud of their group memberships, for example, being a volunteer or being an employee. This identity-based boost to one's esteem comes from perceiving members of dissimilar groups as "outgroup" individuals who possess lower status and less desirable characteristics than members of the focal group. Within nonprofits, there is a danger that paid employees view volunteers as out-group members and less valuable to the organization than other employees. Scarier still is the possibility that even a nonprofit's leaders and supervisors—as employees—could view volunteers as lower-status human resources for the organization and treat them accordingly.

Simpson (1996) captured such realities in a comparison of volunteer and paid firefighters working alongside one another in combination fire stations. Although volunteer firefighters outwardly displayed their pride by putting on bumper stickers that read "Paid or Volunteer, We're All Professionals" and were quick to minimize status differences between themselves and paid firefighters, employee firefighters often dismissed their volunteer firefighter counterparts as unreliable, inept, and not of the same caliber. Smith (1994) noted that nonprofit employees sometimes resent volunteers because organization managers frequently make employees "watch" volunteers or take on the added responsibility of supervising them and their work without correspondingly enhancing the employee's compensation. Nonprofit managers also sometimes hold paid staff responsible for work mistakes that volunteers make (Pearce, 1993). Taken together, volunteer and employee identity-based group dynamics have the potential to tank workplace relations, and ultimately volunteer engagement, if nonprofit leaders do not proactively create a positive organizational climate that values the contributions of volunteers.

How do visions of constructive volunteer-employment relations become a reality? As with work design, the seeds of volunteer engagement and constructive volunteer-employee workplace relations must be cultivated before the first volunteer steps foot in the organization. Volunteer involvement must be articulated in a nonprofit's strategic plans. Guiding documents should be clear about how all types of human resources, including volunteers, will contribute to the agency's actualization of its vision, mission, and core values. Next, leaders and managers should have a clear operational plan for how volunteers will be integrated into the larger workforce. Organization charts should include volunteer positions or, at the very least, roughly conceptualize where and how volunteers will be used to augment and support departments or organizational objectives. The placing of volunteers ought not to be an ad-hoc, last-minute exercise. If it is, and if volunteer assignments and tasks are not thought out prior to a volunteer arriving, there is a higher likelihood that strained volunteer-employee relations will follow. As for paid employees (to include a nonprofit's leaders or managers), they ought to know and understand the role of volunteer participation in the organization, how volunteer contributions are critically important for the organization's success, and what role (if any) employees will play in onboarding, training, developing, or interacting with volunteers. Employees are more likely to constructively partner with volunteers, as opposed to viewing volunteers as a burden or even as competition, if they are meaningfully involved in planning for the arrival of volunteers.

Once volunteers join a nonprofit, managers must actively cultivate workplace harmony and constructive volunteer-employee relationships. Leaders must be aware of how volunteers are feeling and what challenges they might be encountering in their interactions with employees. Leaders must also be mindful not to make decisions that inadvertently burden employees and cause paid staff to resent the presence of volunteers, such as blaming them for errors that volunteers cause or asking them to take on volunteer administration-related responsibilities without providing them adequate space to perform their regularly assigned jobs. Additionally, messaging, communication, and regularly scheduled meetings can keep volunteers and employees informed of what is happening organization-wide and how members of each group are contributing to goals and objectives. In-person and virtual events can also facilitate social interactions between volunteers and paid staff and foster the development of a team environment within the organization. The key to constructive volunteer-employee workplace relations is to reduce "in-group, out-group" identity-based dynamics and instead get everyone in the organization rowing in the same direction, with the same intensity, and toward a shared goal. Only then can a nonprofit capitalize on positive relationships and enhance volunteer engagement.

Recognition and Rewards

Have you offered praise or rewards to your organization's volunteers within the past seven days? Hopefully, your answer is a resounding "YES!" If it is not, do not feel bad or beat yourself up over it. Instead, consider how you might do so within the next seven days, and then make it happen! A 2016 analysis by Gallup found that only one-third of workers surveyed received praise from their supervisors or organization leaders within the past seven days. Further, many respondents reported that their work accomplishments were routinely ignored altogether. Organizations in all sectors too often miss this relatively straightforward and low-cost engagement opportunity, and it has dire potential consequences—workers who feel inadequately recognized are twice as likely to leave their organizations within a year.

Poor recognition practices are a direct precursor to worker disengagement. This is especially true for an organization's best and highest performers. High work performance is not only the result of high-quality individual knowledge and capabilities but also an individual's *motivation to perform* at a high level of output. There are countless workplace examples of very intelligent people not contributing all that much to organizational performance, or worst yet, causing interpersonal or organizational strife. So, attracting smart individuals or people with certain backgrounds or occupational titles is not enough to guarantee they will be excellent volunteers. Volunteers need to both be *able* and *willing* to do a job well in order for high work performance to occur. In the academic study of human resource management, the Ability-Motivation-Opportunity or AMO model (Jiang et al., 2012) is used to describe this not-so-straightforward relationship between performance ability and willingness. The third dimension beyond *ability to perform* and *willingness to perform*, the *opportunity to perform* or the "O" in the AMO model, describes how managerial and HR practices can provide pathways for high-quality work performance to emerge and contribute to organizational effectiveness. As it relates to volunteers and nonprofits, offering recognition and giving out rewards are important practices that set the stage for engagement. Praise reinforces a sense of accomplishment among volunteers and validates their reason for participating. It helps to remind them why they chose to donate their time and talent in the first place and centers the volunteering experience within one or more of the psychological needs that involvement is intended to fulfill—altruism and a desire to give back, personal growth and self-esteem development, career development, or whatever else. Even more to the point, recognition and rewards let volunteers know that they are doing great work for their organization. One's knowledge that they are performing well in the workplace is correlated to satisfaction, and satisfaction at work is related to one's continuing effort to perform their work (Lawler & Porter, 1967). Praise for contributions well-done kick-starts a virtuous cycle among volunteers in which they become explicitly aware of how their efforts are making a difference for others and within themselves, experience satisfaction from being involved, and become even more motivated to perform assignments well and leverage their skills in service to the nonprofit and its clients.

Suggestions abound about how to effectively recognize and reward volunteers. Points of Light, an international nonprofit devoted to engaging volunteers to help solve societal problems, suggests sending electronic "thank you" cards and giving volunteers "shout outs" that specifically mention their names and cite specific contributions, using internal (e.g., newsletters or bulletin boards) and external (e.g., social media) communication channels to engage in volunteer storytelling, providing service awards that mark achievement milestones (such as hours served or volunteering anniversaries), and hosting in-person and virtual team recognition events to celebrate volunteer contributions. Other ideas from a variety of sources include offering spot rewards and tokens of appreciation (such as movie tickets or gift baskets), an annual volunteer appreciation gala, letters of appreciation gathered from the organization's clients or community members, giving out personalized merchandise or organizational "swag" (such as a coffee tumbler with the nonprofit's logo and the volunteer's name), having a dedicated volunteer blog or website, frequent and routine volunteer check-in calls or visits, periodic snacks and refreshments, a volunteer suggestion box, hosting events that volunteers' families can attend and participate in, providing recommendation letters or endorsements, creating photobooks or public displays of volunteer involvement, feature volunteers in organizational interviews and public media, and hosting "victory parties" to celebrate specific organizational accomplishments, among others. Equally important for nonprofit leaders and managers is creating what Gallup (2016) calls a "recognition-rich environment" in which genuine praise is frequent, comes from every direction, is aligned with an organization's purpose, and reflects what the organization aspires to become for itself and to others. The key here is to ensure that praise does not become empty and disingenuous. Instead, nonprofits must seek to create an honest organizational culture that regularly acknowledges and appreciates volunteer contributions.

Conclusion

This chapter discussed the various ways nonprofit organizations and leaders can enhance volunteer engagement. Volunteers are a critical human resource for just about every nonprofit agency and community organization. They extend the capabilities and reach of organizations and enable them to better serve clients. In order to understand volunteer engagement, we first considered why volunteers donate their time and talents in the first place. Having a good grasp of the complex motivations that fuel volunteerism is a necessary first step in effectively engaging volunteers. Among various explanations, the desire of individuals to fulfill psychological needs is a powerful force behind the intent to volunteer. Individuals volunteer to facilitate personal growth and understanding, satisfy emotional needs, develop career networks, learn new knowledge and skills, interact with friends, and give back to their communities and society. Knowing this, nonprofit leaders can leverage human resource and organizational practices to strengthen the connection between volunteer involvement and personal need fulfillment. These practices include creating volunteering opportunities that bring individual and organizational values into alignment, designing volunteer assignments in meaningful ways, providing continuous learning and development opportunities, building a positive work climate that enables constructive volunteer-employee relationships to flourish, and establishing a recognition-rich environment that regularly and genuinely acknowledges the contributions and impact of volunteers. Once these and other engagement-enhancing nonprofit leadership strategies become commonplace in an organization, volunteer engagement will surely follow.

REFERENCES

Allen, N. J., & Rushton, J. P. (1983). Personality characteristics of community mental health volunteers: A review. *Nonprofit and Voluntary Sector Quarterly*, *12*(1), 36–49.

American Psychological Association. APA Dictionary of Psychology. https://dictionary.apa.org/psychology

American Sociological Association. What is Sociology? https://www.asanet.org/about/what-sociology

Auslander, G. K., & Litwin, H. (1988). Sociability and patterns of participation: Implications for social service policy. *Nonprofit and Voluntary Sector Quarterly*, *17*(2), 25–37.

Bell, W., & Force, M. T. (1956). Urban neighborhood types and participation in formal associations. *American Sociological Review*, *21*(1), 25–34.

Berger, G. (1991). Factors explaining volunteering for organizations in general and for social welfare organizations in particular. Unpublished doctoral dissertation, Heller School of Social Welfare, Brandeis University.

Bobo, L., & Gilliam, F. D. (1990). Race, sociopolitical participation, and black empowerment. *The American Political Science Review*, *84*(2), 377–393.

Chacko, T. I. (1985). Member participation in union activities: Perceptions of union priorities, performance, and satisfaction. *Journal of Labor Research*, *6*(4), 363–373.

Clary, E. G., Snyder, M., Ridge, R. D., Copeland, J., Stukas, A. A., Haugen, J., & Miene, P. (1998). Understanding and assessing the motivations of volunteers: A functional approach. *Journal of Personality and Social Psychology*, *74*(6), 1516.

Cook, C. E. (1984). Participation in public interest groups membership motivations. *American Politics Research*, *12*(4), 409–430.

Curtis, J. E., Grabb, E. G., & Baer, D. E. (1992). Voluntary association membership in fifteen countries: A comparative analysis. *American Sociological Review*, *57*(2), 139–152.

Dearlove, D., & Coomber, S. (1999). Heart and soul and millennial values. Skillman, NJ: Blessing/White.

Florin, P., Jones, E., & Wandersman, A. (1986). Black participation in voluntary associations. *Nonprofit and Voluntary Sector Quarterly*, *15*(1), 65–86.

Freeman, R. B. (1997). Working for nothing: The supply of volunteer labor. *Journal of Labor Economics*, *15*(1), S140–S166.

Gallup. (2010). The business case for well-being. https://news.gallup.com/businessjournal/139373/Business-Case-Wellbeing.aspx

Gallup. (2016). Employee recognition: Low cost, high impact. https://www.gallup.com/workplace/236441/employee-recognition-low-cost-high-impact.aspx

Hackman, J. R., Oldham, G., Janson, R., & Purdy, K. (1975). A new strategy for job enrichment. *California Management Review, 17*(4), 57–71.

Hager, M. A., & Brudney, J. L. (2004). Volunteer management practices and retention of volunteers. The Urban Institute.

Hodgkinson, V. A., & Weitzman, M. S. (1986). The charitable behavior of Americans: A national survey. Independent Sector.

Hodgkinson, V. A., Weitzman, M. S., Noga, S. M., & Gorski, H. A. (1992). Giving and volunteering among American teenagers 12 to 17 years of age. Independent Sector.

Hougland, J. G., Jr., & Christenson, J. A. (1982). Voluntary organizations and dominant American values. *Journal of Voluntary Action Research, 11*(4), 7–26.

Jiang, K., Lepak, D. P., Hu, J., & Baer, J. C. (2012). How does human resource management influence organizational outcomes? A meta-analytic investigation of mediating mechanisms. *Academy of Management Journal, 55*(6), 1264–1294.

Lawler, E. E., III., & Porter, L. W. (1967). The effect of performance on job satisfaction. *Industrial Relations: A Journal of Economy and Society, 7*(1), 20–28.

Lemon, M., Palisi, B. J., & Jacobson, P. E. (1972). Dominant statuses and involvement in formal voluntary associations. *Nonprofit and Voluntary Sector Quarterly, 1*(2), 30–42.

Musick, M. A., & Wilson, J. (2007). Volunteers: A social profile. Indiana University Press.

Palisi, B. J., & Korn, B. (1989). National trends in voluntary association memberships: 1974–1984. *Nonprofit and Voluntary Sector Quarterly, 18*(2), 179–190.

Palmer, K., & Blake, D. (2018). The expertise economy: How the smartest companies use learning to engage, compete, and succeed. Nicholas Brealey Publishing.

Pearce, J. L. (1993). *Volunteers: The organizational behavior of unpaid workers.* Routledge.

Pew Research Center. (2019). The generations defined. https://www.pewresearch.org/fact-tank/2019/01/17/where-millennials-end-and-generation-z-begins/ft_19-01-17_generations_2019/

Points of Light. (2021). 4 ways to recognize volunteers and keep them engaged. https://www.pointsoflight.org/blog/4-ways-to-recognize-volunteers-and-keep-them-engaged/

Posner, B. Z., Kouzes, J. M., & Schmidt, W. H. (1985). Shared values make a difference: An empirical test of corporate culture. *Human Resource Management, 24*(3), 293–309.
Qualtrics. (2022). Employees who feel aligned with company values are more likely to stay. https://www.qualtrics.com/blog/company-values-employee-retention/
Robert Half. (2018). The importance of upskilling your employees. https://www.roberthalf.com/blog/management-tips/the-importance-of-upskilling-your-employees
Senge, P. (1990). *The fifth discipline. The art & practice of learning organization.* Doubleday/Currency.
Simpson, C. R. (1996). A fraternity of danger. *American Journal of Economics and Sociology, 55*(1), 17–34.
Smith, D. H. (1994). Determinants of voluntary association participation and volunteering: A literature review. *Nonprofit and Voluntary Sector Quarterly, 23*(3), 243–263.
Snyder, M., Clary, E. G., & Stukas, A. A. (1999). The functional approach to volunteerism. In why we evaluate (pp. 377–406). Psychology Press.
Tajfel, H., & Turner, J. C. (2004). The social identity theory of intergroup behavior. In political psychology (pp. 276–293). Psychology Press.
Turner, J. C. (1987). *Rediscovering the social group: A self-categorization theory.* Blackwell.

CHAPTER 6

Boards & Engagement: Spectrum of Involvement

The role of a nonprofit's board of directors on the engagement of its employees cannot be ignored. In much the same was as senior leadership can affect the engagement of employees in for-profit firms, nonprofit BODs in that senior leadership role have an influence—be it indirectly through the Executive Director or directly depending on the level of involvement. Let's use the analogy of two somewhat controversial parenting trends—the "free-range" parent v. the "helicopter parent." The "free-range parent" is one who tends to allow children to have more independence and generally tries to provide less direct supervision (Morin, 2021; Skenanzy, 2008). They are not neglectful; rather, they view their role as helping the child to build their own independence safely. For nonprofits, this may look like a board of directors that is consistent in their meetings, board activities, etc. However, when it comes to the actual running of the organization, they prefer to remain more hands-off so as to allow the organization to independently operate, work out its own concerns, etc. On the other hand, the "helicopter" parent is very involved and tends to provide constant direct supervision and guidance (Ginott, 1969). For nonprofits, this may look like a board of directors that is "micro-managing"—perhaps even in attempts to be helpful and provide guidance—but essentially preventing the organization from performing independently of the board. While nonprofits certainly are not comprised of children, these terms can act as starting points to help categorize the approach a board of directors may take at each extreme.

Free-Range   Helicopter

The "Free-Range" Board: Lack of Ecosystem Knowledge

The board's involvement in the nonprofit's activities may vary along a spectrum from completely hands-off to highly involved. Each of those extremes poses its own set of challenges, with the "perfect" level of involvement lying somewhere in the middle. For boards that are not involved at all, instead choosing to leave all activities to the Executive Director, several concerns are present. First, an uninvolved board runs the risk of not understanding the broader ecosystem in which the nonprofit operates. Members may not understand the stakeholders of the organization—funders at all levels, clients, partners, etc. This lack of knowledge regarding ecosystem may translate into a larger misunderstanding about why the organization has a specific set of needs or "asks." A BoardSource 2021 Leading with Intent survey of 820 nonprofit Executive Directors and Board of Directors Chairperson reported a disconnect between the grade given for an overall understanding of the context in which the organization is working—in other words, its ecosystem. Executive Directors gave a C + for this facet of involvement, while BOD Chairs graded themselves at a B-. Neither grade is particularly encouraging. Let's consider an example of how a lack of involvement leads to neglect for the nonprofit's broader ecosystem.

Imagine this scenario: A child advocacy center where children alleged to have been abused in some manner are interviewed by trained forensic interviewers to provide a statement to the necessary child protective services, law enforcement, prosecutorial, etc. parties. The board of this particular agency is essentially hands-off when it comes to the organization. They show up once a month for meetings, vote on whatever the Executive Director instructs, approve documents with the cursory review, and the like. At one such meeting let's imagine the Executive Director approaches her board asking for soundproof paneling for an interview room. The board is confused—isn't the interview room at one end of the hallway and the facility's waiting room at the other? Why would the paneling be needed? Is this a necessary expense, or a responsible use of funds? This out-of-ordinary request is one the uninvolved board does not have the capacity of properly assessing because they don't understand the organization's functions—they haven't witnessed those functions or attended staff meetings to get a sense of how loud the waiting room can get during an interview, or to recognize that you can hear children who speak loudly or cry during their interviews. This is indicative of a lack of knowledge regarding the very ecosystem of the organization. As an employee leader of the organization, the Executive Director may feel frustrated with their board's lack of involvement and disappointed in its response to their request.

If you're reading this from a for-profit perspective, the aforementioned situation would be analogous to a company's board not understanding key facets of the environment when the CEO presents them. But employees at all levels feel the board's lack of involvement as well. For example, boards of directors who fail to understand the ecosystem of the organization may also not recognize the need for certain policies or procedures to protect their employees and/or enhance their professional development and well-being. Consider how this may affect even the most important of tasks like setting pay structures. A board of directors that understands the nonprofit's environment would stay informed as to salary survey data from nonprofits in similar sub-sectors and geographical locations in order to ensure employee pay was competitive and that living wages were offered.

The "Free-Range" Board: Lack of Everyday Knowledge

Boards can also fail to be involved in the nonprofit's everyday operations, with its own deleterious consequences. According to a 2021 Leading with Intent survey, Board Chairs and Executive Directors graded the commitment and involvement of their Board of Directors at a B-. This has perhaps the most devastating consequences for organizational culture. The influence of top leadership on organizational culture cannot be denied, nor can the link between culture and a host of organizational outcomes—satisfaction, performance, etc. The role of the board is to help the Executive Director create a culture that leads to engagement. For example, does the board support (both in concept and financially in practice) efforts to care for and recognize employees? Seemingly simple ideas of this abound—does the board sign thank you notes and birthday cards for employees? Does the board understand the organizational chart of the organization and, more importantly, understand the name and responsibilities of each individual fulfilling a particular position? Do they promote respect in their treatment of the Executive Director and employees by role modeling empathy and kindness in their interactions and by supporting the Executive Director in holding accountable those who may mistreat employees? Boards can also play an important role in the diversity, equity, and inclusion initiatives at the organization, both by supporting such initiatives and by participating in them where appropriate. Does the board encourage recruiting and selection practices that are not only legal (lowest minimum bar) but also equitable for all candidates? Does the board encourage the nonprofit's staff to be reflective of its client population, recognizing that those served will feel more comfortable if they can see themselves in the employee population? Does the board itself purposefully recruit and retain members who are *also* representative of the staff so as to make employees feel as included as clients served? These efforts also translate into more engaged employees. We know that when people feel included, they are more engaged in their work, more creative, etc. Despite the known benefits of purposeful diversity, equity, and inclusion, 62% of Executive Directors surveyed reported that their BODs do not spend enough time on a commitment to equity.

An uninvolved board also runs the risk of simply not understanding enough of what the organization does to be its advocate in other stakeholder settings. For example, one nonprofit asked its board members to carry a laminated card with the organization's mission, vision, and key points on it in case they ran into a stakeholder of the organization. That seems a low bar for a board of directors—perhaps they should actually know those things, without a physical prompt? This way, when they're engaged in formal networking or even just informal conversation and an opportunity to speak about the amazing work of the nonprofit arises, they are ready! This impacts the nonprofit's current employees because everytime a board member speaks about the organization; they are either helping to enhance or detract from its brand. In turn, this also affects the ability of the organization to recruit and retain the best employees. It's difficult to be engaged in your organization when it is associated with negativity (Liu et al., 2015).

Lastly, an uninvolved board likely doesn't know the actual activities its employees are performing. In one food pantry, the Board of Directors helped work pantry shifts alongside employees. This gave them first-hand knowledge of how clients signed up to shop at the pantry as well as the process for greeting them and helping them select groceries. It allowed the board to see what federal guidelines were in place regarding nutrient requirements v. what clients actually selected. Such participation also allowed for board members to see where unique situations occurred and even to experience such situations themselves. For example, how to help clients who were on foot or bicycle select and package groceries, what to say to clients who couldn't get a time to shop but still showed up needing assistance, how important it is for clients to have access to foods that align with their religious and cultural preferences, etc. These board members now understood why the organization was asking for a better scheduling database, improved lighting in the pantry, and on-site translators for non-English-speaking clients. Perhaps most importantly, board members got to experience first-hand the skill set necessary to do this important work. Board meetings following that experience had a different tone, one that translated into more supportive employment practices. Those practices in turn enhance employee engagement.

The Helicopter Board: Members as Agents of Barrier Creation

Before you reach the conclusion that board member involvement is the best thing for employee engagement, let's focus on the other end of the spectrum—the helicopter board. This type of involvement is what may be termed the "dark side.' Let's discuss what effects such over involvement may have on employee engagement. First, too much daily involvement can create a lack of independence and autonomy for employees at all levels. Executive Directors may internalize the over involvement as a lack of trust and/or confidence in their abilities, leading to a decrease in engagement, satisfaction, etc. Overinvolvement on the board's part may neutralize the role of the Executive Director. In extreme situations this may lead to an organization in which employees bypass the director altogether and seek the input of the board directly. The Executive Director in such a situation would have little to no reason to remain engaged with the organization. Such overinvolvement may also introduce issues of power dynamics. If the board is too overly involved in daily operations, employees may feel caught in between the Executive Director and the BOD, particularly in instances where the two disagree. Essentially, this creates a toxic culture in which everyone feels disengaged and dissatisfied. Such cultures are prime for employee turnover.

Consider these results: the previously mentioned Leading with Intent survey (conducted in 2021) also asked both Executive Directors and Boards of Directors to evaluate board performance based on board strategy. The two strategies were strategic and operational. The aforementioned "free range" board likely has neither area of focus. They lack both strategic and operational purposes and goals. For our purposes, the overinvolved board (or 'helicopter' board) is more likely to have an operational focus—an extreme focus on everyday issues to the detriment of more strategic purposes. Results of the survey indicated that both Executive Directors and BOD Chairpersons rated the board's performance higher when the board had a strategic v. operational focus. This tells us that Executive Directors and the board's leadership both find that an overly involved board is less likely to perform well. Since the board's overall performance has trickle down effects on the performance of the nonprofit and on its employees via messaging in policies and practices approved by the Board of Directors and via their role in helping establish the organization's culture, it seems reasonable to infer that an optimal level of board involvement may be a strategic focus (Fig. 6.1).

In the next section, let's take a look at the differences between the three board archetypes, and visually consider an overall depiction of the effects of board involvement on employee engagement.

Fig. 6.1 Continuum of involvement

1. The Approach and the Effects

Below is a simplified table explaining the three approaches a Board of Directors may take in its role (Table. 6.1).
Let's visually consider what each approach may look like in terms of employee engagement:

As you can see, neither over involvement nor under-involvement are likely to translate to positive engagement outcomes, but for different reasons. A large part of the board's role when it comes to employee engagement is conveyed via messaging, either direct or indirect, consciously or subconsciously. Free-range boards are signaling a lack of care for employees. When they fail to understand the ecosystem within which the nonprofit operates, and/or don't comprehend the direct service activities employees are responsible for on a daily basis, the signaling is one of neglect. It is important to note here that the message interpretation is what matters, not necessarily the intention of the board. It may be that the board truly values the employees of the organization. However, it is just as important that such messages of value and support be conveyed. On the other hand, a helicopter board may believe they are signaling care and value by being overly involved. Yet the message signaled to employees is one of distrust (Fig. 6.2).

Table 6.1 Three approaches to involvement

Free-Range	Strategic	Helicopter
Members lack knowledge of operational activities at all	Members understand operational activities and have participated first-hand; they are not involved everyday	Members are overly involved in everyday direct client operations of the nonprofit
Members are not a source of support and guidance for the Executive Director	Members act as a sounding board for the Executive Director in both operations and employment areas	Members neutralize the role of the Executive Director by being too present for other employees
Members don't prioritize DEI initiatives among BOD, Executive Directors, and other employees	Members prioritize their own DEI and encourage the Executive Director to do the same	Members are overly involved in the recruitment and selection process of general employees

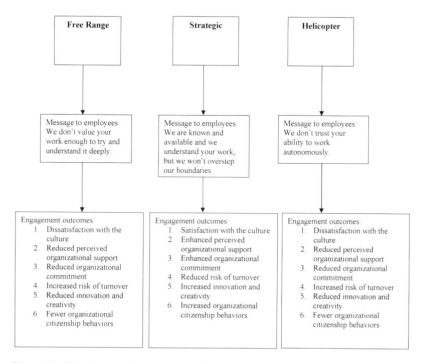

Fig. 6.2 The Approach-engagement link

We acknowledge that being just involved enough so as to create positive employee engagement without being so involved as to negatively affect employees is a delicate balancing act, one that most boards likely have yet to master. In the next section, let's practically consider how boards may strike such a balance.

WHAT DOES A "STRATEGIC" BOARD ACTUALLY DO?

In a 2021 Stanford Social Innovation Review piece on "purpose-driven board leadership," Anne Wallestad suggests that boards adopt a different mindset for thinking about themselves and their relationship with the organization. Such a purpose-driven mindset consists of 4 principles: (1) Purpose before organization; (2) Respect for ecosystem; (3) Equity mindset; (4) Authorized voice and power. We will rely on these as a guide in describing how a strategic board may function.

Purpose Before Organization

First, a board intent on creating an environment that ultimately serves to enhance employee engagement is one that first focuses on the organization's fundamental purpose—why does it exist in the first place? This shift requires the board to shift from considering what's best for the nonprofit itself to asking what is best for the grand challenge the organization is working to address. Such a pivot requires the board to consider stakeholders external to the organization and assume a role of allocating organizational resources in ways that serve those stakeholders. This mindset creates a dialog as boards seek to make an impact on the cause, not just keep the organization running. Involving internal stakeholders (like employees) in such discussions is likely to engage them creatively, perhaps in a way in which they haven't been engaged previously. After all, employees often join nonprofits because of commitment to a cause, not necessarily commitment to any one organization operating within that cause. In turn, we know that the recognition of employees as an important internal stakeholder because of their connection to the ultimate stakeholder—clients served—results in more engaged employees.

For example, consider the food bank organization mentioned previously. While the organization's board of directors would not be classified as strategic in every sense of the word, it does do a good job of focusing on the core purpose behind the organization—feeding hungry people. Along those lines, it listened to feedback from social workers who noted that many of their clients were homebound and could not venture out to pick up food, particularly during the COVID pandemic. The board heard this feedback and turned to its front line employees for help brainstorming what could be done to ensure that this particular population of hungry clients received the food they needed. The employees, eager to be involved in solving this problem, came up with a simple solution. The warehouse had two large doors that were accessible for incoming deliveries of donated food. In addition, there was also a smaller, regular-sized door for warehouse staff and volunteers to enter and exit. Employees surmised that by putting a shelving unit nearest to the regular door, they could create pre-packaged food bundles and leave them out for social workers specifically to pick up for clients. This didn't interrupt the regular process for obtaining food—social workers instead called on behalf of their clients and scheduled a "warehouse pickup," which was then specifically created by warehouse staff as part of their daily sorting duties. The door was always unlocked during regular business hours, so social workers could estimate a time of arrival to ensure the pack was ready but were otherwise able to come into the warehouse and pick up the bundle with their client's name on it. A small refrigerator was also placed near the shelving to include perishable portions of the bundle.

A board focused solely on the organization's sustainability may not have recognized the importance of this handful of external stakeholders who could not participate in the traditional procedures for obtaining food. But this board recognized that its purpose was at stake if it could not adequately feed hungry people in the community. And so, it turned to its most knowledgeable resource—its employees—to serve that purpose in a more creative way. In doing so, it empowered its employees and welcomed their creativity, resulting in increased employee engagement.

Respect for Ecosystem

Next, a board of director recognizes that the nonprofit it is guiding is part of a broader network of organizations with similar purposes. Earlier, we spoke about ecosystem in terms of understanding all of the organization's moving parts and their relationships with one another. But the strategic board is focused even beyond that—they think of the nonprofit organization as part of an open system and recognize that its actions have reverberations on the broader nonprofit community and beyond, on the cause itself. They also recognize that these actions will eventually affect the engagement of their own employees. For example, let's consider a nonprofit that focuses on the mental health of child victims of abuse. These "victim advocates" are an intensely trained group of mental health professionals that are available essentially round-the-clock to respond to immediate mental health concerns. In addition, they also provide one-on-one counseling in traditional office settings. Currently these professionals also sit on a number of multi-disciplinary teams (MDTs) in order to provide their input—they may provide professional opinions to law enforcement, child protective services, prosecutors, etc. The organization is considering applying for a sizeable grant that would allow it to create smaller satellite offices to house advocates as opposed to a centralized model. The satellite offices would reduce the amount of travel time advocates spend getting to and from immediate response calls, arguably opening up the time available for standardized counseling appointments. In addition, the use of satellite offices would allow for the organization to provide longer periods of off time for advocates. It could conceivably close entire satellites for several consecutive days and shift workload to other locations. The board feels this would be a particularly important benefit, as they are committed to the prevention of employee burnout.

Certainly, the board of directors in this position deserves commendation for recognizing the gains to be had by guiding the Executive Director to apply for this grant, particularly in trying to protect its employees from increased commute time and burnout. However, a strategic board of directors would also look beyond the immediate gains of its organization to consider how the changes may impact other organizations. It may begin collecting information from the organizations with which its advocates work frequently—suppose the data from those partner agencies points out that it appreciates the centralized advocate model because all of the advocates on staff are briefed on all cases, a benefit that would likely diminish or entirely be removed if a satellite model was in place. Partner agencies may also point out that the closure of satellite offices would create a situation in which advocates unknown to partner agencies were common, particularly in instances of turnover where a victim advocate may be hired into this new model and thus only ever associated with a certain location. These affected agencies might recognize that the burnout rate of such mental health advocates is certainly high and that care should be taken to protect these caregivers—however, they would also point out that the importance of a consistent presence is also undeniable for victims trying to recover from trauma. Such feedback may not have occurred to a board of directors without the strategic mindset in place to consider the broader ecosystem in which the organization lives. Ultimately, the feedback from partner agencies also has an effect on employee engagement. Should the board of directors choose to support the application of a grant for satellite offices, particularly given this feedback, employees may find the atmosphere of their MDT meetings less positive. They may begin to feel rejected by the partner agencies. Long-term, such dissatisfying relationships with partner agencies may lead to less engagement in their roles—the organization must decide if this is a fate similar to, better than, or worse than the burnout they were trying to avoid in the first place!

Equity Mindset

The strategic board is committed to diversity, equity, and inclusion—but in a deeper manner than just hiring statistics or publicizing the demographics of clients served would suggest. This is a board that questions how its very programs and processes for accessing those programs may be situated in systemic inequities. Let's consider our food bank organization again. This organization's board is wrestling with significant and deep-seated questions related to its founding and procedures for obtaining food. Founded as part of a church program in the 1980s, the organization eventually grew into its own separate nonprofit, though its past is still visible in the organization's name (Loaves & Fishes) as well as its volunteer base (primarily white senior citizens of mid-upper socioeconomic status). Recently, as part of its strategic planning efforts, a group of employees brought up the notion that part of planning for the organization's future meant asking difficult questions regarding its roots and current operations. For this organization, that meant asking itself about the proverbial notion of a "white savior complex." The organization's board looked a lot like its founders and volunteer base, which was not representative of its client population. Further, the ties to religion begged questions of inclusivity—did people in need recognize that the organization served people of all religious affiliations, including those with no particular affiliation at all?

A traditional, well-meaning board would have paid some level of attention to these questions, but the strategic board in this example went to new levels in grappling with them. This board undertook a massive surveying of its current clientele, questioning them about how the organization made them *feel*, not just about their satisfaction with the food received. Recognizing that many of its clientele held a distrust of the system, surveys were anonymous and demographic data was only collected where it was deemed vital to the survey results. More importantly than the survey data, employees began holding coffee and breakfast conversation groups and inviting clients to share in a small yet open forum their opinions of the organization and ideas for a path forward. It was important that all this work was completed by employees with the most face-to-face interaction with long-term clients—many of them already had relationships of trust established, which increased their willingness to share. In fact, while the board of directors recognized the necessity of such forums for discussion, they purposefully did not attend so as not to disrupt the camaraderie between clients and employees. Clients were told that the information would be shared with the board anonymously, and indeed employees did present to the board a summary of the results from both the survey data and coffee sessions. The board then folded this information into their strategic planning process, leading them to consider a re-brand of the organization and an increased attention to ensuring that clients saw themselves in the employees and volunteers with whom they interacted. While much work remained, the board had at least taken steps to questioning its history as it considered its future.

How does this translate into increased employee engagement? Well, in heeding the call by employees to address the organization's current equity mindset and involving employees in efforts to hear from the clients themselves, the organization demonstrated its commitment to employees and trust in their opinions—a message that translated into enhanced engagement!

AUTHORIZED VOICE AND POWER

This hallmark of a strategic board is, at its heart, about board composition. Who comprises the board of directors is one of an organization's most important questions. A poorly-composed board may prove toxic to the organization, while a high-functioning board could lead to optimal impact on not just the organization, but its ecosystem of partner agencies as well as the cause itself. While a traditional board may consider what "we" think is best for the organization, a strategic board questions who comprise the "we" and questions its own composition. Consider the board at a nonprofit whose cause is free or reduced fee access to reproductive medical care. This is a nonprofit that, by definition of its mission, is likely to serve more individuals identifying as female v. male. This is also an organization that is likely to serve individuals from a lower socioeconomic status, given its focus on free or reduced care costs. Would it make sense for such an organization to have a board of directors composed primarily of individuals identifying as male who hold professional careers as doctors, lawyers, etc.? If you're considering this question from the point of view of a traditional board, you may be arguing that such a board composition is exactly what the organization needs—imagine the fundraising potential and campaigns about allyship! But if you're the demographic most likely to utilize the services of this organization, consider how seeing the faces of the Board of Directors would make you feel. This is where a strategic board mindset comes into play. And statistics surrounding strategic boards with this mindset are concerning. According to BoardSource's 2021 survey of Executive Directors, 49% reported not having the board members in place that would help establish trust within the communities served by the organization. Relatedly, only 32% of boards reported that it was important to have knowledge of the community served, and 28% agreed that actual membership in the community being served was important.

A strategic board gives power to those who are affected by board governance by putting them on the board itself. Imagine the empowerment felt by that same demographic if individuals see themselves represented in the organization's guiding body. Imagine the engagement this creates for employees—to work for an organization that thinks strategically about who should be on its board and that gives voice to those who perhaps have not previously been in positions of authority. Employee engagement is enhanced by board composition because when employees recognize the care and effort a board takes to cultivate its membership, they are proud of the organization. Further, they are more likely to benefit from such care in decision-making themselves, as it seems unlikely that a board so invested in the selection of its membership would then ignore its employees. Given that 78% of board members and 87% of Executive Directors are white, 99% are cisgender, and 94% heterosexual (Leading with Intent survey response data), it isn't just giving voice on the Board of Directors that matters—giving voice in the hiring of general employees to those unlike these strikingly similar demographics is also going to be key to enhancing employee engagement.

All told, employee engagement is a tricky concept. Perhaps even more so in the nonprofit sector, as reasons may joining the organization may vary from traditional for-profit employment, as unpaid volunteers work alongside paid employees, and as boards who are mostly themselves unpaid volunteers struggle with the "right" level of involvement. This chapter provides some guidance on the pitfalls of the two extremes when it comes to involvement, and draws from recent literature to present a mid-spectrum third option, the strategic board. Below, we provide additional opportunities for engaging with this chapter's material.

> **Engage with This Chapter**
>
> Part I: Identify a nonprofit organization that you are interested in learning more about. Reach out to the organization and try to find out answers to the following questions:
>
> 1. How involved (or uninvolved) is the board of directors in the organization's regular operations?
> 2. What does the board of directors do to try and enhance the engagement of the organization's employees?
>   a. If such activities exist, is there evidence that they are successful?
>   b. If such activities do not exist, is there justification for why not?
> 3. Does the organization attempt to measure employee engagement?
>
> Part II: Based on your reading of this chapter as well as the information provided by the organization, where would you place the organization on the spectrum of involvement? What suggestions would you provide the organization concerning their current engagement efforts?

References

Ginott, H. G. (1969). Between parents and teenager, NY:AVdn.
Leading with Intent. (2021, June). BoardSource Index of Nonprofit Board Practices.
Liu, G., Chapleo, C., Ko, W. W., & Ngugi, I. K. (2015). The role of internal branding in nonprofit brand management: An empirical investigation. *Nonprofit and Voluntary Sector Quarterly, 44*(2), 319–339.
Morin, A. (2021, September 26). "The Free-Range Style of Parenting," https://www.verywellfamily.com/
Skenazy, L. (2008, April 1). "Why I Let My 9-Year-Old Ride the Subway Alone". *The New York Sun.* https://www.nysun.com/
Wallestad, A. (2021, March 10). The four principles of purpose-driven board leadership. *Stanford Social Innovation Review.*

CHAPTER 7

Community Engagement: Beyond These Walls—Boards and Social Innovation via Advocacy

WHAT IS ADVOCACY?

The role of the board within the nonprofit is certainly key to its mission, vision, and ultimate sustainability. But a nonprofit's Board of Directors can have an impact on the organization externally as well, in the form of community engagement—also known as advocacy. In fact, many theorists argue that advocacy is among the most important functions of nonprofit organizations, because such organizations are often the closest to disenfranchised groups and may be able to act as conduits between public policy and local communities (Boris & Krehely, 2002; Kimberlin, 2010; Salamon, 2002). More specifically, board involvement in advocacy is frequently identified as a key role or responsibility of a nonprofit board member (Axelrod, 1994; Carver, 1990; Drucker, 1992; Houle, 1989; Iecovich, 2004; Soltz, 1997). BoardSource explains advocacy in terms of three broad kinds: (1) Sharing the mission. In this type of advocacy, board members act as ambassadors to the organization. They purposefully share and communicate the mission of the organization and its activities to others. This includes public stances of support and (when needed) defense of the nonprofit's mission. (2) Lobbying. Advocacy surrounding lobbying can be confusing for nonprofit organizations. In the case of boards, lobbying would involve a board member or members acting on behalf of the organization to express a view or opinion on a specific piece of legislation and issue a call to action regarding the legislation.

It's important to note that several activities in which board members may participate are not considered lobbying. For example, (a) Board members can publicly engage in self-defense lobbying if the nonprofit's existence is threatened. (b) Board members can act as private citizens and not as representatives of the organization. Lastly, board members can engage in political activity acting on behalf of the nonprofit, but must remain nonpartisan so as not to threaten the organization's 501c (3) status. As with lobbying, board members can act as private individuals if they choose to take sides and engage in partisan campaigning. If board members do choose to act as private citizens in the case of either lobbying or partisan political activity, this should be made clear so as not to harm the nonprofit. Skidmore (1999) suggests that boards actually "institutionalize their advocacy strategies," making advocacy part of the board's strategic plan for the organization (Iecovich, 2004, p. 7).

Shier and Handy (2015) use the innovation in nonprofit literature to craft their three-part typology for social change efforts made by nonprofit organizations. Recognizing that not all innovations are socially driven, their work specifically considers ways in which nonprofits seek to create social change—such social innovations are defined as "any new idea with the potential to improve either the macro-quality of life or the quantity of life," and macro-quality of life is defined as "the set of valuable options that a group of people has the opportunity to select" (p. 22584, original source Pol & Ville, 2009, p. 882). In their conceptualization, the group of people refers to those accessing the services provided by the nonprofit. In other words, social innovations are undertaken by nonprofits to positively affect the lives of those they serve, either in quality, quantity, or both. Such changes must be significant as well, so as to create fundamental change. For Shier and Handy (2015), advocacy falls under the first of three social innovations, socially transformative social innovations. These include both political advocacy as well as public awareness initiatives. In a follow-up study, Shier and Handy (2016) identify board involvement as key to social innovation efforts of the organization. Boards must be focused on social change, engaged with key stakeholders, and perhaps even form board subcommittees devoted to advocacy and awareness. It was important to the authors that advocacy not just be considered political efforts to sway issues, but that the focus be on real social innovation instead. We acknowledge, therefore, that advocacy is a specific type of social innovation undertaken by boards to create positive change for the stakeholders of their organizations.

While 43% of nonprofit executive directors and 42% of board chairs report that outreach efforts, including acting as ambassadors for the organization's mission are among the top three board functions most in need of improvement, whether and how nonprofit boards decide to engage in community advocacy depends on many factors, including the composition of the nonprofit's funds. Board members may actively share the mission of the organization with potential funders as a way to build relationships. However, in the case of more strident lobbying and/or political activities, it may seem counterproductive to criticize an entity (for example, government) that the organization also appeals to for funds. In their meta-analysis of the factors relating to a nonprofit's overall engagement in advocacy, Lu (2018) identified board support as among the top two factors (the other being knowledge of laws) positively associated with advocacy. In other words, boards of directors who endorse advocacy and are themselves advocates lead organizations that advocate for themselves as well.

Unfortunately, while the argument can certainly be made that advocacy efforts should be a top priority for nonprofit boards, the truth is that oftentimes the professionalization of nonprofits and the focus on internal governance may lead to neglect of these broader social innovations.

QUALITIES OF A BOARD MEMBER ADVOCATE

Vandeventer (2011) referred to advocacy as "civic reach," and explains that in addition to fundraising and governance skills, civic reach is the third ability of a great board member. Vandeventer (2011) recommends nonprofits consider the following three functions of civic reach in recruiting and selecting new board members: (1) the personal and professional prestige of the potential member; (2) the knowledge of local goings-on held by the potential member, and (3) the connections the potential board member can leverage to create communitywide or even worldwide relationships for the nonprofit. Taken together, these three factors make up a board member's civic reach. But board members with civic reach also possess four other qualities that make them important to the organization, according to Vandeventer (2011). These include (1) "Shrewd environmental sensing." This refers to a board member's knowledge about unfolding information and can assist the nonprofit in positioning itself in such a way so as to capitalize on events-yet-to-occur in a way that positively impacts both the agency and those they serve, not just sharing mission but expanding its reach. (2) The credibility to stand up for the nonprofit's mission. This refers to a board member's leverage in the community with decision makers, such that their voice would be heard and heeded. (3) The ability to reach the broader public. Board members with this quality have connections not only with decision makers, but also roots and relationships in the communities the nonprofit is trying to serve. (4) Inside access to power. This refers to a board member with the ability to connect organizations with those making resource allocation decisions.

Building on these characteristics to practically understand how civic engagement may occur, Matthews (2020) recently identified four central themes describing how board chairs could participate in nonprofit civic engagement. However, these could easily be extended to the entire board as a whole. The themes are as follows: (1) Representing constituents. This includes attempts by the board to involve all relevant stakeholders. (2) Facilitating participatory processes. This may include actions like (a) organizing community forums that are accessible for stakeholders of the cause and/or organization. One board member described this facilitation as "Boards have another role; it's being the voice of the community on public policy issues" (p. 206). (3) Engaging in civic governance. This includes the use of political influence by board members to advocate on behalf of their organizations. (4) Organizing community and developing leaders. In this role, boards facilitate relationships among those in the community that care about the same issue. Creating such connections can also serve as a sort of succession planning for board members; identifying those with leadership potential may assist in filling vacant board positions at a later time.

In their book, *Forces for Good: the Six Practices of High-Impact Nonprofits* (Grant & Crutchfield, 2007, 2012) came to the conclusion that what nonprofits do outside of their own organizations to create such collective impact matters more than their own internal capabilities. The six practices they identified require boards of directors with qualities like those mentioned above. Let's discuss each in turn and the role a board member may play:

1. Serve and advocate. According to Grant and Crutchfield (2007, 2012), all high-impact organizations eventually divide their efforts between direct client services and advocating for real social

change for those they serve. Advocacy requires boards with knowledge of the organization's ecosystem, as well as the leverage and abilities required to influence that ecosystem to create positive social change.
2. Make markets work. The high-impact nonprofits identified by Grant and Crutchfield (2007, 2012) recognize that not all people are motivated solely by altruism, but instead understand that some appeal to self-interest may be necessary to cultivate social change. These nonprofits work within the existing market system—perhaps by using their influence to change business behaviors (perhaps by partnering with large business to help them reach underserved markets), establishing corporate partnerships that help to bring in monetary and/or in-kind donations, publicity, etc., or even through the creation and maintenance of their own side businesses to generate funds for direct client services. Because board members are often members of the local business community, they can serve as a bridge between for-profit, market-driven business and the organization's programs.
3. Inspire evangelists. In this sense, evangelists is used by Grant and Crutchfield (2007, 2012) to refer to those fervent supporters of the organization who are able to "convert" outsiders to become supporters as well. By this definition, all board members should be evangelists for the organization, bringing in outsiders and helping them create connections with the organization such that those outsiders then become supporters themselves.
4. Nurture nonprofit networks. High-impact nonprofits recognize that collaboration is key to advocacy. They work together instead of engaging in funding competition. This strengthens their influence and improves the likelihood of creating positive social change. Board members who understand their role as organizational advocates with an eye toward influencing change will embrace this collaborative mindset, perhaps even utilizing their own connections to identify potential collaborators for their agency.
5. Master the art of adaptation. In order to be a high-impact nonprofit that is cultivating positive social change, organizations must be able to adapt. The ability to both try something new and have a plan for assessing its degree of success or failure is something that boards can guide.

6. Share leadership. The nonprofits studied by Grant and Crutchfield (2007, 2012) built out strong boards of directors that willingly shared leadership responsibilities with executive teams as well as outside collaborators. These high-impact boards were also larger— ranging in size from 20 to 40 or more individuals.

Taken together, the idea that nonprofits are impactful because of their external influence (v. their internal operations) and the fact that all six of these principles involve strong boards with individual advocates serving underscores the importance of the board of directors in community advocacy.

Barriers to Boards' Advocacy Efforts

Although advocacy may be one of a nonprofit's most important roles, and while boards may agree that it is a top three priority needing improvement, this does not mean advocacy comes easily. Figure 7.1 visually represents the board characteristics that may be preventing nonprofit boards from becoming better advocates for their organizations, as discussed in Smith and Pekkanen (2012).

The first concern, size of the board, is really a structural issue. Boards that are smaller in size may feel the constraints of including advocacy as part of their priorities. Organizations should purposefully consider the size of their board of directors to better support the ability of boards to advocate, perhaps by increasing the number of board members to the point that subcommittees focused on advocacy as well as other board priorities could form.

The second constraints may be felt in the forms of decreased capacity and/or motivation to advocate based on the volunteer nature of a board of directors. These can be addressed in the "Tips for Beginning" steps below, either as part of board member onboarding or in a separate, specialized advocacy training.

Perhaps the most interesting (and more difficult to alleviate) barriers may lie in the beliefs of the members themselves. In order to effectively advocate, boards must include all stakeholders—remember, they are not only advocating for the organization, but for its stakeholders. This will require boards to abandon the notion that stakeholders do not know what is best for themselves and their communities. Kanagasingam's (2018)

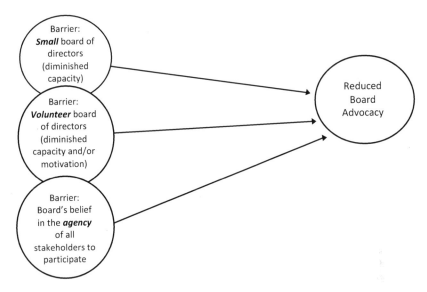

Fig. 7.1 Barriers to Advocacy

human-centered design process may be a good first step for boards that find themselves dealing with their own biases regarding their stakeholders.

Tips for Beginning

When it comes to engaging with stakeholders, boards may be uncomfortable or nervous. Fiona Kanagasingam (2018) outlines a process of human-centered design (HCD) that may be helpful in bridging the gaps between what the board envisions being a stakeholder is like v. the actual lived experience of one of the organization's constituents. The process of "journey mapping" consists of 5 steps that allow board members to "map" the lived experience of the community members its organization serves.

1. Entice. In this first step, it's important to understand how those served first hear about the organization. How do they feel? Are they scared or hopeful? What do they want that they think the organization can help them gain?

2. Enter. What are first interactions like in your organization? Who is/are the first points of interaction between stakeholders and the organization?
3. Engage. What are the highlights and challenges of the organization, as seen by its stakeholders? These may be both first-interaction based as well as sustained opinions formed after multiple interactions.
4. Exit. What is it like for stakeholders when they stop relying on the organization for specific services? Who do they talk to? How do they feel?
5. Extend. What do stakeholders tell others about their experiences with your organization? In the same way your board members are advocating for the organization, so are de facto ambassadors to the organization being created in clients. What will their message be to others in the community?

The idea behind HCD is that by understanding the lived experiences of the organization's stakeholders, boards can better understand in what direction to drive social innovations.

BoardSource's "Stand For Your Mission" campaign was created in 2014 as a way to educate boards on the importance of advocating for their organizations, and providing practical tips for doing so. According to their publication, board advocacy has three main components:

1. Strategy. This involves an understanding of how the environment surrounding the organization could impact its work. It includes purposefully creating paths that allow the organization to seize opportunities while addressing potential environmental threats. In this role, advocacy is leveraged as a way to "get things done."
2. Budget & Resources. In this role, the board is responsible for having a clear understanding of how the organization is funded, including areas of vulnerability if public policy shifts.
3. Personal engagement. Board members should leverage their personal influence to support the organizations advocacy needs—this may include setting up meetings and/or town halls with key stakeholders, making calls, etc.

According to BoardSource, the ability to advocate for the organization should be part of each board member's responsibility. In fact, they encourage nonprofit boards to consider the following questions in order to maximize advocacy:

1. Do board members understand that advocacy is an expectation? Is this written into the role description for board members?
2. Do we hold onboarding training or guidance for new board members to help them understand how we engage in advocacy efforts, including how we expect them to act as ambassadors for our mission?
3. Do we understand the networks of our board members such that we can pull from those personal connections when needed?
4. Is our board representative of a broad cross-section of our stakeholders?
5. How does our board member recruitment strategy help or hinder advocacy efforts?

Outcomes

Advocacy efforts by board members should contribute to the updated version of collective impact outlined by Kania et al. (2022). According to the authors, centering equity within collective impact involves the following:

1. **Grounding the work in data and context, and targeting solutions.** This directly reflects the human-centered design approach discussed earlier in the beginning advocacy steps. As lived experiences are mapped, organizations can focus on specific solutions with a better understanding of the context surrounding the issues with which the organization engages.
2. **Focus on systems change.** This relates to advocacy for social innovation as outlined by Shier and Handy (2015). Particularly when collective impact is focused on equity, addressing the root causes of a social issue requires systemic dismantling of long-held beliefs and systems.
3. **Shift power within the collaborative.** As Matthews (2020) suggested, the inclusion of all stakeholders is necessary for positive advocacy that creates collective impact. The role of the board is to

ensure not just the representation of diverse stakeholders, but to act as facilitators in creating inclusive spaces for discussion.
4. **Listen to and act with community.** Board members cannot advocate for a community they do not know and understand. Advocacy that leads to collective impact requires deep trust by communities. Boards must build that trust alongside their organizations by physically and mentally showing up and engaging in the communities served by their organizations.
5. **Build equity leadership and accountability.** In order to advocate in such a way so as to create collective impact, board members must accept accountability for ways in which they individually, or the organizations they represent, are failing to be equitable.

Future Considerations

As boards recognize and embrace the need to engage in advocacy to assist their organizations in creating positive social change, there are additional considerations for the future of this work. First, much of what we have covered above is based on research activities and experiences of U.S.-based nonprofits. Yet so many of the world's most complex "grand challenges" are not bound by geographical guidelines. Let's consider the United Nations' 17 Sustainable Development Goals (SDGs).

Source: un.org/sustainabledevelopment/

In fact, all of the SDGs are complex problems because they are not bound to any one specific country. Instead, they affect us all—as evidenced by goal #17, partnerships for the goals. To pretend that climate change, poverty, food insecurity, etc. are problems that can be solved by the advocacy of even the most powerful nonprofit being led by the most influential board is naïve at best, and egotistical at worst. Instead, we must investigate how community advocacy is performed by boards in nonprofit organizations or their like across the globe and then use this information to ascertain how such boards can encourage international advocacy. The SDGs take the viewpoint that we are all really one big community—board advocacy practice and the research that informs it should do the same.

Relatedly, a second consideration involves technology and advocacy. Advances in technology mean that any organization can publicize their advocacy efforts to everyone with access to internet. This should make the partnerships necessary to advocate across international boards more practical. However, enhanced technological platforms also raise questions about board members' level of comfort in using such forums for advocating for their organizations. According to BoardSource's most recent Leading with Intent report (June 2021), 61% of board members representing the organization surveyed were age 45 or older while 28% were 44 or younger (1% unknown age). This runs counter to social media usage by age, with 86% of Millennials (those born between 1981 and 1986) reporting the use of social media, and decreasing social media use by age. Simple possession of a smart phone, social media use aside, also has a negative correlation with age. 93% of Millennials own a smartphone, compared to 90% of Gen Xers (born 1965–1980), 58% of Baby Boomers (born 1946–1964), and 40% of the Silent Generation (born 1928–1945) (Dimock, 2019; Vogels, 2019). The use of technology can enlarge the reach of advocacy available to nonprofits. For example, when organizations recognized an opportunity to advocate for support to reauthorize the Violence Against Women (VAWA) Act, they leveraged social media networks using the hashtag '#realVAWA' to share personalized stories from survivors and explain to the public how the reauthorization of VAWA could provide for victims otherwise left vulnerable. In addition, advocates were able to stay connected via conference and video messaging calls, emails, etc. (Brescia, 2020). But given the statistics regarding the age of boards, we know that many organizations currently have boards of directors who are (a) less likely to own a smartphone, and (b) less likely to use social media. Certainly, a smartphone is not the only method by which a board member could engage publicly in a way to benefit their organization, but it may arguably be the fastest. Beyond that, even if a board member does have a smartphone, they may not know how to engage in social media. All this is to say that organizations should make it a point to understand the comfort level of their boards in the use of technology for community advocacy. It may be that board members require training to enable them to use online platforms to advocate on behalf of the organization.

Lastly, nonprofits (and the boards that advocate for them), must think about how advocacy efforts changed as a result of COVID. For example, arts organizations were unable to hold annual galas. What did they do to pivot instead so as not to lose donors—did they take to social media to champion their cause, etc.? What of these changes will remain in a post-pandemic world? How have boards adapted, and how must they continue to adapt to ensure the needs of their stakeholders are heard in a time when the world is recovering from the single-most important disaster of our lifetimes?

Taken together, this chapter has outlined what advocacy may look like for different organizations, considered the qualities of nonprofit organizations and individual board members that are effective in advocating for their stakeholders, outlined the barriers to advocacy board members may face and ways to address those, and discussed what the future of advocacy may hold for boards. Below, we offer some practical exercises for further engaging with this chapter.

> **Engage with This Chapter**
>
> Part I: Identify a nonprofit organization that you believe is doing a good job of advocating for its organization's mission and stakeholders (provide evidence of effective advocacy and define the advocacy type). Reach out to the organization and try to find out answers to the following questions:
>
> 1. Describe the organization's board of directors (size, descriptive statistics, etc.)
> 2. What methods of advocating do board members utilize?
> 3. Are board members trained in advocacy? Is it outlined as a clear expectation during the member recruiting and selection phase?
> 4. Are there barriers to continued/enhanced board advocacy? What are these (be specific).
>
> Part II: Based on your reading of this chapter, what suggestions would you make to the organization to address the barriers identified above? If no barriers are identified, what plans would you draft for the organization to help enhance current advocacy efforts?

> **Engage with This Chapter**
>
> Identify a nonprofit organization that you believe is *not advocating effectively* for its organization's mission and stakeholders (provide evidence of ineffective advocacy and define the advocacy type). Research the organization and its advocacy movement, and answer the following:
>
> 1. Based on your research and in your opinion, what factors are preventing the nonprofit from effective advocacy?
>   i. Can you tell to what extent the board is or is not involved in the organization's advocacy efforts?
>   ii. What characteristics of the board may be affecting the advocacy efforts?
> 2. What would you recommend for improving the ability of the organization to advocate?

REFERENCES

Axelrod, N. R. (1994). Board Leadership and Board Development. In R. D. Herman & Associates (Eds.), *The Jossey-Bass handbook of nonprofit leadership and management* (pp. 119–136). Jossey-Bass.

BoardSource, (2016, June 8). *What is advocacy?* https://boardsource.org/resources/what-is-advocacy/

BoardSource, n.d. *The power of bard advocacy: A discussion guide for boards.* https://boardsource.org/research-critical-issues/stand-mission-advocacy/

Boris, E., & Krehely, J. (2002). Civic participation and advocacy. In L. Salamon (Ed.), *The state of nonprofit America* (pp. 299–330). Brookings Institution Press.

Brescia, R. (2020, June 30). How Technology Shapes Social Movements. *Stanford Social Innovation Review.*

Carver, J. (1990). *Boards that make a difference: A new design for leadership in nonprofit and public organizations* (pp. 130–148). Jossey-Bass.

Crutchfield, L. R., & Grant, H. M. (2012). *Forces for good: The six practices of high-impact nonprofits.* John Wiley & Sons.

Dimock, M. (2019, January 17). *Defining generations: Where Millennials end and Generation Z begins.* Pew Research Center.

Drucker, P. F. (1992). *Managing the nonprofit organization: Principles and practices.* Harper Collins.

Houle, C. O. (1989). *Governing boards: Their nature and nurture* (pp. 89–95). Jossey-Bass.

Iecovich, E. (2004). Responsibilities and roles of boards in nonprofit organizations: The Israeli case. *Nonprofit Management and Leadership, 15*(1), 5–24.

Kanagasingam, F. (2018, February 21). Using human-centered design to advance civic engagement in nonprofits. *Stanford Social Innovation Review.*

Kania, J., Williams, J., Schmitz, P., Brady, S., Kramer, M., & Juster, J. (2022, Winter). Centering equity in collective impact. *Stanford Social Innovation Review.*

Kimberlin, S. E. (2010). Advocacy by nonprofits: Roles and practices of core advocacy organizations and direct service agencies. *Journal of Policy Practice, 9*(3–4), 164–182.

Lu, J. (2018). Organizational antecedents of nonprofit engagement in policy advocacy: A meta-analytical review. *Nonprofit and Voluntary Sector Quarterly, 47*(4_suppl), 177S–203S.

Leading with Intent. BoardSource Index of Nonprofit Board Practices. June 2021 report.

Mathews, M. A. (2020). The embeddedness of nonprofit leadership in civic governance. *VOLUNTAS: International Journal of Voluntary and Nonprofit Organizations, 31*(1), 201–212.

Pol, E., & Ville, S. (2009). Social innovation: Buzz word or enduring term?. *The Journal of Socio-Economics, 38*(6), 878–885.

Salamon, L. (2002). Explaining nonprofit advocacy: An exploratory analysis. Johns Hopkins University, Institute for Policy Studies, Center for Civil Society Studies Working Paper No. 21.

Shier, M. L., & Handy, F. (2015a). From advocacy to social innovation: A typology of social change efforts by nonprofits. *Voluntas: International Journal of Voluntary and Nonprofit Organizations, 26*, 2581–2603.

Shier, M. L., & Handy, F. (2016). Executive leadership and social innovation in direct service nonprofits: Shaping the organizational culture to create social change. *Journal of Progressive Human Services, 27*, 111–130.

Skidmore, E. (1999). Board Leadership 2000: Critical Roles for the New Century. In N. Ehrlich-Finklestein & R. Schimmer (eds.), *The new board: Changing issues, roles and relationships* (pp. 1–18). Haworth Press.

Smith, S. R., & Pekkanen, R. (2012). Revisiting advocacy by non-profit organisations. *Voluntary Sector Review, 3*(1), 35–49.

Soltz, B. A. B. (1997). The board of directors. In T. D. Connors (Ed.), *The Nonprofit handbook: Management*. Wiley.

Vandeventer, P. (2011, Spring). Increasing civic reach. *Stanford Social Innovation Review*.

Vogels, E. (2019, September 9). *Millennials stand out for their technology use, but older generations also embrace digital life*. Pew Research Center.

CHAPTER 8

Measuring Engagement: Theoretical Perspectives and Practical Approaches

By now, it is clear that highly engaged and committed nonprofit stakeholders—employees, volunteers, boards of directors, and community members—can enhance productivity, innovation, performance, service outcomes, and local and global impact. What is less clear is how exactly to measure whether employees are indeed engaged and meaningfully contributing to a nonprofit organization's mission and objectives in measurable ways. A report by Harvard Business Review Analytic Services notes that "while most executives see a clear need to improve employee engagement, many have yet to develop tangible ways to measure and tackle this goal" (2013, p. 1).

A common refrain for why measuring engagement is so difficult is that there is little consensus about what engagement truly is. Many scholars and practitioners might agree that engagement has some relation to, say, workplace satisfaction, commitment, involvement, loyalty, passion, energy, motivation, enthusiasm, or performance. But precisely how these and other ideas are related to the construct of engagement has been up for debate since the introduction of the concept of engagement itself. Schaufeli and Bakker (2010) contend that "no agreement exists among practitioners or scholars on a particular conceptualization of...engagement" (p. 11). This might explain Attridge's (2009) contention that "most companies...are not measuring employee engagement" (p. 386).

Unfortunately, we cannot resolve this decades-old dilemma in the space of this chapter (nor would we be able to do so within the space of the entire book). Instead, our goal is to provide nonprofit organizations and leaders with actionable guidance for measuring, enacting, and sustaining workplace engagement. We do this by first summarizing several scientific, theory-based academic surveys that are frequently used to measure engagement in work organizations. These include the Utrecht Work Engagement Scale (UWES), the Gallup Q12 Employee Engagement Survey, and three surveys by May and colleagues (2004), Rich and colleagues (2010), and Saks (2006) that are grounded in psychology theory and literature. Understanding the theoretical, research-based, evidence-backed origins of engagement and its measurement helps set the stage for and legitimizes effective practical application.

Next, we expand beyond purely scholarly conceptualizations of engagement to consider what engagement might look like in everyday practice. That is, what sorts of employee and organizational behaviors and outcomes might indicate to nonprofit leaders and managers that engagement is present within their organizations. We will discuss job satisfaction, employee productivity and performance, turnover rates and intention to stay, organizational identification, commitment and loyalty, organizational citizenship behaviors, and counterproductive workplace behaviors. Lastly, we introduce several ways managers and leaders can periodically gauge workplace engagement, including via the use of annual engagement or climate surveys, pulse surveys, Employee Net Promoter Score (eNPS) analysis, focus groups, 1-on-1 "check-ins," exit interviews, "stay" interviews, and dashboards and scorecards.

THEORY-BASED, SCIENTIFIC APPROACHES TO MEASURING ENGAGEMENT

Utrecht Work Engagement Scale

The Utrecht Work Engagement Scale (UWES)—so named due to its founders being affiliated with Utrecht University in The Netherlands—is "one of the most widely used instruments for measurement of engagement" (Shrotryia & Dhanda, 2019). It is based on the work of Schaufeli and colleagues (2002) and incorporates a definition of engagement that considers one's vigor, dedication, and absorption at work. *Vigor* refers to energy level and an employee's willingness to persist when performing work tasks. *Dedication* involves having a sense of pride and enthusiasm about one's work. *Absorption* is characterized by an employee's focus and concentration in the workplace; the workday passes quickly when absorption is high. The original survey contained 17 items (or questions), and a shorter 9-item version was created a few years after the original (Schaufeli et al., 2006). Table 8.1 lists some example questions from the UWES as well as from the other academic surveys of engagement presented in this section.

Gallup Q12 Employee Engagement Survey

The scientific knowledge that contributed to the validation of the Gallup Q12 Employee Engagement Survey, also known as the Gallup Workplace Audit (GWA) or simply the Q12, in the late 1990s began decades earlier with the research of Dr. George Gallup and University of Nebraska psychologist Dr. Don Clifton (Harter et al., 2020). A notable difference between the UWES and Q12 approach to measuring engagement is that the Q12 measures job resources which can become antecedent to engagement, as opposed to actual individual engagement. As Schaufeli and Bakker (2010) explain, "the Q12 assesses the perceived level of resources in the employee's job and not his or her level of engagement. As such, rather than the *experience* of engagement in terms of involvement, satisfaction, and enthusiasm, the *antecedents* of engagement in terms of perceived job resources are measured" (p. 15). In Chapter 4, we described how certain organizational dynamics and leadership actions can serve as job resources that enable the creation of employee engagement. The Q12 measures these resources that give rise to workplace engagement. Gallup has statistically linked their measures of (the antecedents of) engagement and outcomes such as job satisfaction, productivity, retention, loyalty, and profitability through multiple studies cumulatively involving millions of workers in over 100 countries (Schaufeli & Bakker, 2010; Shrotryia & Dhanda, 2019).

The Effect of Meaningfulness, Safety, and Availability on Engagement

May and colleagues (2004) developed a 13-item survey that measures the cognitive, emotional, and physical dimensions of employee engagement. Building on the work of Kahn (1990), who is credited as "the first scholar who conceptualized engagement at work" (Schaufeli & Bakker,

Table 8.1 Selected academic approaches to measuring employee engagement

Scientific, Evidence-Based Surveys of Engagement	Sample Survey Questions
The Utrecht Work Engagement Scale (Schaufeli et al., 2002)	• At my work, I feel that I am bursting with energy • Time flies when I'm working • When I get up in the morning, I feel like going to work • My job inspires me • At my work I always persevere, even when things do not go well Items are measured on a 7-point scale ranging from "never" to "always"
Gallup Q12 Employee Engagement Survey, also known as the Gallup Workplace Audit (GWA) or simply the Q12 (Harter, Schmidt, Agrawal, Blue, Plowman, Josh, & Asplund, 2020)	• Do you know what is expected of you at work? • Do you have the materials and equipment you need to do your work right? • In the last seven days, have you received recognition or praise for doing good work? • Does your supervisor, or someone at work, seem to care about you as a person? • In the last year, have you had opportunities at work to learn and grow? Items are measured on a 5-point scale ranging from "strongly disagree" to "strongly agree"

Scientific, Evidence-Based Surveys of Engagement	Sample Survey Questions
Meaningfulness, Safety, and Availability (May et al., 2004)	• Performing my job is so absorbing that I forget about everything else • I am rarely distracted when performing my job • I really put my heart into my job • Time passes quickly when I perform my job • My own feelings are affected by how well I perform my job • I exert a lot of energy performing my job Items are measured on a 5-point scale ranging from "strongly disagree" to "strongly agree"
Value Congruence, Perceived Organizational Support, and Core Self-Evaluations (Rich et al., 2010)	• I work with intensity on my job • I devote a lot of energy to my job • I am enthusiastic in my job • I am proud of my job • I am excited about my job • At work, my mind is focused on my job • At work, I am absorbed by my job Items are measured on a 5-point scale ranging from "strongly disagree" to "strongly agree"
Job Versus Organizational Employee Engagement (Saks, 2006)	Job Engagement Items • I really "throw" myself into my job • Sometimes I am so into my job that I lose track of time • This job is all consuming; I am totally into it • I am highly engaged in this job Organizational Engagement Items • Being a member of this organization is very captivating • One of the most exciting things for me is getting involved with things happening in this organization • Being a member of this organization makes me come "alive" • I am highly engaged in this organization Items are measured on a 5-point scale ranging from "strongly disagree" to "strongly agree"

2010, p. 12), their inquiry into engagement considers how meaningful it is for one to bring themselves into the "performance" of work (meaningfulness), how safe it is for them to do so (safety), and to what extent they have the physical and psychological bandwidth to do so (availability). Items such as "I really put my heart into this job" and "I exert a lot of energy performing my job" are measured on a five-point scale, with respondents indicating their level of agreement with each statement.

The Mediating Effect of Value Congruence, Perceived Organizational Support, and Core Self-Evaluations on the Engagement-Performance Link

Rich and colleagues (2010) also build on the meaningfulness, safety, and availability dimensions of engagement originally proffered by Kahn (1990), but include the psychological variables of value congruence, perceived organizational support (POS), and core self-evaluations to more fully explain the complex relationships between individual perceptions, organizational dynamics, and workplace engagement. Value congruence describes a situation where the workplace behaviors that an organization expects of its workforce are aligned with an employee's own self-image. Such alignment heightens one's perception of meaningfulness. POS occurs when employees perceived that their employer cares about their well-being and values their efforts. Feelings of psychological safety follow perceptions of organizational support. And core self-evaluations—or one's confidence in their capabilities, effectiveness, and worthiness—prompt people to become more psychologically and even physically available at work due to them feeling more poised to do great work. Taken together, higher ratings of value congruence, POS, and core self-evaluations lead to greater engagement and, subsequently, positive individual and organizational outcomes. Rich and colleagues' (2010) survey is comprised of 18 engagement items rated on a 5-point scale from "strongly disagree" to "strongly agree."

Job Versus Organizational Employee Engagement

The final academic study we cover in this section was one of the first to differentiate between an employee's engagement with their job and their engagement with their work organization. Saks (2006) believed that workers could distinctly be "present" (or not) in either their job, their organization, or both, and investigated the organizational dynamics that give rise to each of these conditions. His research uncovered that POS predicts both job and organizational engagement, while job characteristics (such as task significance and autonomy) specifically predict job engagement, and organizational justice perceptions predict one's engagement with their organization. A five-item scale was developed to measure job engagement, and a six-item scale measured organizational engagement. Saks (2006) found that job and organizational engagement predicted such outcomes as job satisfaction, organizational commitment, intention to quit, and discretionary effort or organizational citizenship behaviors (that is, engaging in behaviors beyond one's formal job responsibilities, such as helping a coworker learn a work-related skill).

PRACTICAL OBSERVATIONS OF NONPROFIT ENGAGEMENT: THINGS TO LOOK FOR

Given the lack of consensus about what workplace engagement actually is or consists of, measuring it can be a daunting, if not downright impossible, task for many nonprofit organizations. What are leaders to do if they do not have organizational psychologists on staff who can internally replicate the scientific studies discussed above, or the budget to hire expensive consulting firms to do so for them? In the final section of this chapter, we present several practical methods for assessing engagement. But first, in this section we discuss several "clues" nonprofit managers can look for to get a sense of the level of engagement that exists within their organizations.

Job Satisfaction

Quite simply, employees respond positively when they are happy with the various elements of their workplace—their supervisors and coworkers, their compensation levels and benefits, the fairness of employment policies and procedures, their opportunities for growth and development, and so on. Engaged workers are satisfied workers who feel connected to an organization's mission and values, and as a result of this connection they tend to be absent less frequently and are less likely to leave the organization. Numerous academic studies have demonstrated a statistically significant link between employee engagement, satisfaction, and desired individual, group-level, and organizational outcomes (e.g., Kamalanabhan et al., 2009; Verona et al., 2017; and others). The general satisfaction level of your nonprofit employees can be a powerful indicator of their level of engagement.

The question for nonprofit leaders to ask here is: **"Are our employees satisfied?"**.

Employee Productivity and Performance

Throughout this chapter and indeed the entire book, we have highlighted the link between employee engagement and work productivity and performance. Engaged employees have high levels of self-efficacy and core self-evaluations and are confident in their abilities to perform their work tasks (Rich et al., 2010). Productive employees also tend to have the organizational tools and resources needed to achieve individual and departmental objectives; thus, they have been set up for success by their leaders and organizations. Because of these investments and due to perceptions of having the organization's support, engaged employees are frequently willing to go the extra mile when it comes to serving their employer's clients and customers. When employees are engaged, they contribute positively and effectively to their own performance objectives and the expectations of their organization.

Questions for nonprofit leaders to ask here are: **"Are our employees productive at work?"** and **"Do our employees perform high quality work?"**.

Turnover Rates and Intention to Stay

Engaged employees are committed to their employer and its mission, and workers with the highest levels of organizational commitment are 87% less likely to quit and find another job (Lockwood, 2007). Conversely, disengaged employees perceive poor person-organizational fit with their employer and experience lower levels of meaningfulness in and psychological attachment to their work, which reduces their intention to remain an employee of the organization (Memon et al., 2014). Thus, high turnover rates and having a workforce that constantly thinks about quitting might indicate a lack of employee engagement.

The questions for nonprofit leaders to ask here are: **"If they had the chance to leave and work for another employer, would our employees** choose to stay?" and "Are we experiencing unusually high levels of employee turnover?".

Organizational Identification

When workers are fully engaged in their workplace, they identify with their organization and are personally intertwined with its successes and failures (Kumar & Pansari, 2015). When others say great things about one's employer, employees with high levels of organizational identification take it as a personal compliment. Conversely, these same workers are quick to defend their employers against unfair criticism or negativity. Additionally, identification is positively linked to a host of other correlates of employee engagement, including satisfaction (Karanika-Murray, 2015), perceptions of organizational justice (He et al., 2014), and trust in the organization and its leaders (Srivastava & Madan, 2016). Nonprofit leaders can learn a lot about how engaged their employees and organizational stakeholders are by how strongly individuals identify with the organization and its mission, vision, and values.

A question for nonprofit leaders to ask here is: **"Do our employees and stakeholders see this organization's successes and failures as their own?"**.

Commitment and Loyalty

Employees develop an attachment to organizations for a number of reasons. Sometimes, they form an emotional commitment and want to be part of an organization because membership fulfills emotional needs. At other times, a worker's commitment to their employer reflects a larger attachment to an ecosystem that the employer is part of, such as a local community or a particular city. And sometimes, people feel as though they owe it to the organization or its leaders and people to remain attached. These bases of attachment have been termed affective commitment (I am committed for emotional reasons), continuance commitment (I need to be committed to this place), and normative commitment (I ought to be committed to my organization) (Meyer & Allen, 1991). Since organizational attachment and commitment have been positively linked to employee engagement (e.g., Albdour & Altarawneh, 2014), high levels of organizational commitment can be a signal of an engaged workforce.

A question for nonprofit leaders to ask here is: "**Are our employees committed and attached to the organization?**" Stated more plainly, "**Do our employees want to be here?**".

Organization Citizenship Behaviors (OCBs)

Engaged employees tend not to limit their workplace contributions to the tasks outlined and specified in a job description. Successful work performance depends on employees doing both these specified tasks, duties, and responsibilities (called "task performance" or "in-role performance") as well as activities that are not expressly outlined in a job description but that helps an organization and its people learn, grow, and achieve (called "contextual performance" or "extra-role performance"). These additional discretionary efforts are what scholars call organization citizenship behaviors or OCBs (Borman & Motowidlo, 1997). One frequently-exercised OCB at work is helping behavior, such as when workers help each other learn a new computer system or changes in regulations that will affect how work gets accomplished. Other OCBs include volunteering to serve on organizational committees, providing *constructive* feedback to coworkers and the organization about how to improve processes and outcomes, productively accepting feedback from others and incorporating their suggestions, being punctual at work and not wasting organizational time and resources, and many others. Extra-role behaviors are a key sign that employees are engaged.

A question for nonprofit leaders to ask here is: "**Do our employees do the bare minimum when doing their jobs, or are they sometimes willing to go above and beyond to deliver for the clients and communities we serve?**" Examples of specific questions (adapted from Moorman & Blakely, 1995) that nonprofit leaders can ask themselves when assessing employee engagement levels via OCBs might include:

- Do our employees willingly (and not begrudgingly) provide assistance when their coworkers have questions about how to do something at work?
- Are our employees willing to attend non-work events that are not required but help the organization's image?
- Do our employees regularly meet or beat work deadlines?
- Would our workers defend the organization when outsiders or even other employees criticize it?

- Do our employees show pride when representing the organization in public?
- Is our workforce willing to speak up and honestly express opinions about work-related issues, even if others may disagree?
- Do our employees express genuine concern for and courtesy toward coworkers and supervisors?

Counterproductive Workplace Behaviors (CWBs)

If OCBs describe beneficial behaviors and activities that employees can do at work and that help coworkers and the organization, then the opposite might be characterized as counterproductive workplace behaviors or CWBs. Gruys and Sackett (2003) define CWBs as "any intentional behavior on the part of an organization member viewed by the organization as contrary to its legitimate interests" (p. 30). A wide variety of CWBs have been identified in management scholarship, including excessive absences and tardiness, slow or sloppy work, gossip, aggression and hostility, favoritism, blaming others for one's own mistakes, damaging or destroying organizational property or resources, theft, sabotage, and misuse of information, among many others. The presence of these unproductive and unhelpful behaviors might signal the absence or lack of desired employee engagement.

A question for nonprofit leaders to ask here is: **"Do our employees engage in behaviors that are counterproductive and unhelpful to their coworkers and to the organization?"**.

PUTTING THE ASSESSMENT OF EMPLOYEE ENGAGEMENT INTO EVERYDAY PRACTICE

Creating and sustaining an engaged workforce requires that nonprofit organizations and leaders accurately and effectively assess the drivers and outcomes of employee engagement. In this section, we offer ideas and approaches for regularly accomplishing this important task within nonprofits. Some of these approaches are survey based and involve gathering large-scale data about employee perceptions and behaviors. Annual engagement or climate surveys, pulse surveys, and Employee Net Promoter Score analysis are some examples of survey methods. Other approaches might also collect data from individuals but are more qualitative in nature and designed to produce richer, detailed insights. Exit interviews, so-called "stay" interviews, focus groups, and 1-on-1 check-ins are some examples frequently used by organizations. A third category involves the collection, analysis, and integration of information related to employee engagement. Examples discussed here include dashboards and scorecards. Our aim here is not to provide detailed instructions on how to comprehensively conduct each and every one of these approaches. Rather, we introduce each approach and briefly describe how it contributes to a greater understanding and promotion of individual and organizational engagement.

Survey-Based Methods for Measuring Employee Engagement

Many organizations conduct **annual employee engagement surveys** or **climate surveys** to collect and analyze information about workforce attitudes and practices on a regular and ongoing basis. Doing so allows organizations to gauge how individual realities and experiences compare with organizational strategy, goals, and expectations. Annual surveys also help to establish baseline metrics which can be assessed year over year in terms of performance against benchmarks. Since these surveys are typically conducted only once per year, they tend to be longer and include more questions. A danger with relying solely or primarily on annual surveys of employees, however, is that employee attitudes, behavior, and performance change more frequently than yearly.

One solution to the limited efficacy of annual survey data is the **pulse survey**. These more frequent surveys provide intermittent opportunities for nonprofit leaders to assess engagement. As the name suggests, pulse surveys enable organizations to keep their fingers on the pulse of engagement across time. The topics that feed into pulse survey questions depend on the goal of a particular survey being deployed. Sometimes, pulse surveys are used to periodically measure potential changes in consistent concepts over extended periods of time—satisfaction, commitment, and so on. In other instances, a pulse survey can be utilized to get quick and actionable insights into how employees are responding to a specific change or organizational initiative. Because pulse surveys are conducted much more frequently than annually (e.g., quarterly, monthly, or even weekly or ad-hoc), they should be shorter or much shorter in length than annual engagement or climate surveys. Nonprofit leaders must take care not to induce survey fatigue among employees by administering too many surveys too often.

A popular approach from the world of marketing that is used to measure consumer loyalty—the Net Promoter Score or NPS—is increasingly being applied to the world of work organizations to measure employee loyalty and engagement. First introduced by Frederick Reichheld in a 2003 Harvard Business Review article entitled "The One Number You Need to Grow" that has since been cited more than 4,200 times, the NPS uses a single question to assess performance potential. The question, rated on a scale from 0–10, is: "How likely is it that you would recommend our company to a friend or colleague?" Customers are categorized based on their numerical response as "promoters" (a rating of 9 or 10), "passives" (a rating of 7 or 8), and "detractors" (a rating between 0–6). A company's net promoter score is the overall ratio of promoters to detractors.

The online data management company Qualtrics[1] explains how this concept can be applied to measuring employee engagement. As they note, "**Employee Net Promoter Score (eNPS)** is a tool used to understand how loyal your employees are to the brand" (emphasis added). In the employment context, Reichheld's original question is modified slightly to now ask employee respondents "How likely are you to recommend this company as a great place to work?" Nonprofit leaders can easily replace a company with "nonprofit" or "organization" to make the eNPS more practical for their organizations. The math for the eNPS is the same as for the original tool, with an overall score reflecting the ratio of promoters to detractors.

The idea behind asking customers about whether they would recommend a company to others, or asking employees whether they would recommend others to work for their employer, is that people put their own reputations on the line whenever they promote a company or employer. As such, the proportion of customers or employees willing to take this risk provides useful insight into just how loyal a customer is to a certain brand, or how convinced an employee is that their organization is a great place to work. This tool's simplicity, however, is also a point of contention and caution. As University of Cambridge scholar Zaki and his colleagues (2016) note, "Although the NPS measure can be used as

---

[1] https://www.qualtrics.com/experience-management/employee/measure-employee-engagement/

a loyalty indicator, it does not offer an explanation of the root cause or causes of a low score" (p. 1). Qualtrics offers a similar warning and notes that the "eNPS gives you the **what** but not necessarily the **why**—it does not give you the root cause but the effect of that cause." Nonprofit leaders might look to the eNPS as a starting point for assessing engagement, but much more information would be needed to accurately understand the organization's climate and performance potential.

Qualitative Methods for Measuring Employee Engagement

Deeper and richer engagement insights can be obtained by talking with nonprofit employees—asking them about their experiences, getting them to share their concerns about themselves and others, understanding their perspectives at critical junctures of their careers, and so on. Such qualitative information is not necessarily a substitute for large-scale, quantitative data that is obtained via annual surveys, pulse surveys, and possibly even an eNPS analysis. Instead, gathering discussion-based insights can help nonprofits triangulate multiple perspectives and more comprehensively understand how and why their workforce is or is not engaged.

Similar to how they are often used in marketing research, **focus groups** can help nonprofit leaders gauge important employee engagement-related attitudes and behaviors and the reasons behind such. Bringing workers together periodically provides a vehicle for them to express their voice within the organization, and also allows nonprofits to dig deeper into the antecedents and consequences of employee engagement. Regular supervisor and employee **1-on-1 check-ins** are another powerful information gathering tool at a nonprofit's disposal. In addition to facilitating the development of employee trust in the organization and its leaders, frequent formal and informal check-ins also provide opportunities for workers to discuss sensitive subjects and promote honest conversation.

Two turnover-related qualitative data collection methods include exit interviews and stay interviews. People leave organizations for a myriad of reasons, sometimes preventable and sometimes not. **Exit interviews** allow organization leaders get a better sense of why people choose to leave and what, if anything, could have been done differently to enhance the value proposition of staying in the role. Information gathered during exit interviews has the potential to be especially rich since turnover is oftentimes the end result of a complex interaction between individual, organizational, and environmental factors. Importantly, in the absence of a regular practice of conducting exit interviews, nonprofit organizations may miss clues that point to a need for timely or immediate changes (such as workplace toxicity or a lack of resources that prevents successful job performance). **Stay interviews** attempt to address these and other issues before they come to a head and cause employees to decide to leave. These ongoing, preventative discussions can happen as part of a periodic performance management and facilitation process or at some other regular interval.

Analytic Methods for Measuring Employee Engagement

In addition to gathering primary information via surveys or qualitative approaches, nonprofit organizations and managers can also engage in the routine and ad-hoc collection and analysis of secondary data as part of their efforts to measure and understand employee engagement. As we have discussed throughout the book, there are multiple antecedents and consequences of employee engagement—job resources, employee productivity, the quality of work performance and outputs, workplace safety incidents, absenteeism, turnover, and many more. These and other outcomes and metrics are presumably already part of the organization's inventory of data (though the extent to which organizations curate, clean, maintain, and utilize this information varies widely). For example, organizations should have information on how many employees left the organization in the past year, how much hourly pay or annual salary an employee earns, how many workplace accidents occurred within the past month, or how many clients were serviced by the organization in the past week. **Dashboards, scorecards**, and similar tools can be used to automatically populate, integrate, and update these and other data points into actionable insights for decision-making by nonprofit leaders.

CONCLUSION

Nonprofit organizations need engaged employees and stakeholders in order to effectively serve their clients and communities. While it is clear that engagement is a critical precursor to productive, innovative, satisfied, and achievement-oriented employees, what is less clear is how nonprofit leaders can effectively and realistically measure workforce engagement. Part of this difficulty is owing to the fact that academic literature on what engagement is and how it ought to be measured is fraught with conflicting perspectives. Scientific approaches to measuring engagement such as the Utretch Work Engagement Scale and the Gallup Q12 Employee Engagement Survey are built upon decades of research and psychometric validation, but routinely utilizing these and similar approaches is often unrealistic for all but the largest and most well-resourced nonprofits.

Other, more accessible approaches to assessing engagement within nonprofit organizations focus on identifying and measuring indicators of engagement—things like employee satisfaction, levels of commitment and attachment, worker productivity and performance quality, turnover rates, discretionary effort, and counterproductive behavior. Nonprofit organizations and leaders can utilize tools such as surveys, focus groups and interviews, and dashboards and scorecards to monitor these and other markers of employee engagement and to take active steps toward creating and sustaining a highly engaged workforce.

REFERENCES

Albdour, A. A., & Altarawneh, I. I. (2014). Employee engagement and organizational commitment: Evidence from Jordan. *International Journal of Business*, 19(2), 192.

Attridge, M. (2009). Measuring and managing employee work engagement: A review of the research and business literature. *Journal of Workplace Behavioral Health*, 24(4), 383–398.

Borman, W. C., & Motowidlo, S. J. (1997). Task performance and contextual performance: The meaning for personnel selection research. *Human Performance*, 10(2), 99–109.

Fuller, R. (2014). A primer on measuring employee engagement. *Harvard Business Review*. https://hbr.org/2014/11/a-primer-on-measuring-employee-engagement. Accessed August 24, 2022.

Gruys, M. L., & Sackett, P. R. (2003). Investigating the dimensionality of counterproductive work behavior. *International Journal of Selection and Assessment*, 11(1), 30–42.

Harter, J. K., Schmidt, F. L., Agrawal, S., Blue, A., Plowman, S. K., Josh, P., & Asplund, J. (2020). *The relationship between engagement at work and organizational outcomes*. https://www.gallup.com/workplace/321725/gallup-q12-meta-analysis-report.aspx. Accessed June 14, 2022.

Harvard Business Review Analytic Services. (2013). *The impact of employee engagement on performance*. https://hbr.org/resources/pdfs/comm/achievers/hbr_achievers_report_sep13.pdf. Accessed June 14, 2022.

He, H., Zhu, W., & Zheng, X. (2014). Procedural justice and employee engagement: Roles of organizational identification and moral identity centrality. *Journal of Business Ethics, 122*(4), 681–695.
James, J. B., McKechnie, S., & Swanberg, J. (2011). Predicting employee engagement in an age-diverse retail workforce. *Journal of Organizational Behavior, 32*(2), 173–196.
Kahn, W. A. (1990). Psychological conditions of personal engagement and disengagement at work. *Academy of Management Journal, 33*(4), 692–724.
Kamalanabhan, T. J., Sai, L. P., & Mayuri, D. (2009). Employee engagement and job satisfaction in the information technology industry. *Psychological Reports, 105*(3), 759–770.
Karanika, M., Duncan, N., Pontes, H. M., & Griffiths, M. D. (2015). Organizational identification, work engagement, and job satisfaction. *Journal of Managerial Psychology, 30*(8), 1019–1033.
Kumar, V., & Pansari, A. (2015). Measuring the benefits of employee engagement. *MIT Sloan Management Review, 56*(4), 67.
Lockwood, N. R. (2007). Leveraging employee engagement for competitive advantage: HR's strategic role. *HR Magazine, 52*(3), 1–11.
May, D. R., Gilson, R. L., & Harter, L. M. (2004). The psychological conditions of meaningfulness, safety and availability and the engagement of the human spirit at work. *Journal of Occupational and Organizational Psychology, 77*(1), 11–37.
Memon, M. A., Salleh, R., Baharom, M. N. R., & Harun, H. (2014). Person-organization fit and turnover intention: The mediating role of employee engagement. *Global Business and Management Research, 6*(3), 205.
Meyer, J. P., & Allen, N. J. (1991). A three-component conceptualization of organizational commitment. *Human Resource Management Review, 1*(1), 61–89.
Moorman, R. H., & Blakely, G. L. (1995). Individualism-collectivism as an individual difference predictor of organizational citizenship behavior. *Journal of Organizational Behavior, 16*(2), 127–142.
Reichheld, F. F. (2003). The one number you need to grow. *Harvard Business Review, 81*(12), 46–55.
Rich, B. L., LePine, J. A., & Crawford, E. R. (2010). Job engagement: Antecedents and effects on job performance. *Academy of Management Journal, 53*(3), 617–635.
Saks, A. M. (2006). Antecedents and consequences of employee engagement. *Journal of Managerial Psychology, 21*(7), 600–619.
Schaufeli, W. B., & Bakker, A. B. (2010). Defining and measuring work engagement: Bringing clarity to the concept. *Work Engagement: A Handbook of Essential Theory and Research, 12*, 10–24.

Schaufeli, W. B., Bakker, A. B., & Salanova, M. (2006). The measurement of work engagement with a short questionnaire: A cross-national study. *Educational and Psychological Measurement, 66*(4), 701–716.

Schaufeli, W. B., Salanova, M., González-, V., & Bakker, A. B. (2002). The measurement of engagement and burnout: A two sample confirmatory factor analytic approach. *Journal of Happiness Studies, 3*(1), 71–92.

Shrotryia, V. K., & Dhanda, U. (2019). Measuring employee engagement: Perspectives from literature. *IUP Journal of Organizational Behavior, 18*(3), 26–47.

Srivastava, S., & Madan, P. (2016). Understanding the roles of organizational identification, trust and corporate ethical values in employee engagement– organizational citizenship behaviour relationship: A study on indian managers. *Management and Labour Studies, 41*(4), 314–330.

Verona, A., Simonič, M., & Vlasova, M. (2017). An analysis of the relationship between job satisfaction and employee engagement. *Economic Themes, 55*(2), 243–262.

Zaki, M., Kandeil, D., Neely, A., & McColl-Kennedy, J. R. (2016). The fallacy of the net promoter score: Customer loyalty predictive model. *Cambridge Service Alliance, 10,* 1–25.

CHAPTER 9

Huronia Transition Homes: Employee and Volunteer Engagement for Social Enterprise

Kathy Willis, the Executive Director of Huronia Transition Homes (HTH), does not have any doubt that the main strength of the organization is their employees and volunteers. For over 25 years that she has been with HTH, the employees and volunteers have been the success stories of HTH. Kathy Willis sees her role as leading employees and volunteers who are absolutely dedicated to the survivors. She notes that the employees and volunteers have proved that they are the key to the organization becoming a source of social change in their rural Ontario, Canada, community. They have offered survivors of domestic abuse effective ways to manage the short and long-term effects of mental, and emotional burdens.

After many years of consultation, planning, and analysis, HTH has established a brand-new social enterprise known as *Operation Grow*. Now, Kathy Willis and the leadership team, have big task on their hands. How to develop and implement an effective engagement plan for employees and volunteers of Huronia Transition Homes. They know that engagement is critical to achieving the outcomes of Operation Grow. They are acutely aware that it is one thing to plan a major strategic initiative such as a social enterprise, it is a different ball game for the social enterprise to be effective and sustainable. Kathy Willis is concerned that the enthusiasm of the employees and volunteers will fizzle out overtime without a clear and effective engagement plan that recognizes the unique characteristics of HTH as a nonprofit organization. Also, the engagement plan must take into consideration that HTH is a nonprofit organization that is committed to working to end all violence against all women.

To answer the specific questions related to employee and volunteer engagement, the rest of the chapter provides an overview of HTH and Operation Grow, the social enterprise of the organization.

Huronia Transition Homes (HTH)

Huronia Transition Homes (HTH) was established in 1984 when the need for a safe and secure refuge for women and children was recognized in North Simcoe County. In the following year, La Masion Rosewood Shelter was opened. In the early 1990s, HTH experienced significant growth and expansion within the community. Moreover, the government identified the commitment of the organization to provide services for women and children in the surrounding Simcoe County in both English and Francophone. The core values and the mission of the organization are the key drivers of why it continues to flourish and develop to become a leading player in the nonprofit sector in Simcoe County. HTH established a social enterprise, Operation Grow, which provides employment to clients, further enhance their skills, and provide socio-psychological support. The social enterprise would also enhance other current programs such as Athena's Sexual Assault Counselling & Advocacy Centre and Choices for Children.

Huronia Transition Homes Team

HTH's board of directors consists of a chairperson, a vice-chair, secretary/treasurer, 5 directors, and the executive director. The board of directors and the employees of HTH are committed to providing a positive experience to their clients, as well as assisting clients with their every need in order to heal and reintegrate them back into the community safely.

The management team is made up of Kathy Willis, Executive Director and the following positions, Director of Operations, Manager of Community Relations & Development, and Program Supervisor- La Maison Rosewood Shelter and Choices for Children, Program Supervisor- Athena's Sexual Assault Counselling & Advocacy Centre, Program Supervisor- French Language Services.

SOCIAL ENTERPRISE

A social enterprise is a unique form of organization because it combines multiple objectives. Although, there are different understandings of the activities of a social enterprise, the basic meaning of what constitutes a social enterprise is relatively consistent. "Social enterprises are businesses whose primary purpose is the common good. They use the methods and disciplines of business and the power of the marketplace to advance their social, environmental, and human justice agendas" (Social Enterprise Alliance, USA).

A social enterprise is a business that trades for a social and/or environmental purpose. It will have a clear sense of its 'social mission': which means it will know what difference it is trying to make, who it aims to help, and how it plans to do it. It will bring in most or all of its income through selling goods or services. And it will also have clear rules about what it does with its profits, reinvesting these to further the 'social mission.' (Social Enterprise, UK)

In Canada, a social enterprise is considered to be a business operated by a nonprofit organization. The business provides a product or service to customers and has a defined social, cultural, or environmental value. However, cooperatives and other organizations are also have social enterprises in Canada. Examples of social enterprises include thrift stores, YMCAs fitness centers.

Supported Social Enterprise

A supported social enterprise is a market-based entity founded and supported by a nonprofit organization for the purposes of the economic and social benefit of persons on the social margins who are employed in or trained through the enterprise.

Why Operation Grow

Nonprofit organizations initiate social enterprises for one or more of the following objectives: to provide an additional source of revenue for their social and public services; to provide more service(s) for their clients; to reach more clients in different geographic areas; to respond to specific needs in the community and; to provide employment for their marginalized clients. In addition to the industry specific drivers of social enterprise, Operation Grow was proposed and developed as a result of a number of organizational and external factors.

- One, the results of the focus group of clients included a recommendation that HTH should consider establishing a social enterprise.
- Two, the board of directors identified the need for a multipurpose space.
- Three, the organization has considered the idea to develop a social enterprise with a food option. Four, there is an understanding that women who are survivors are struggling to connect mind and body.
- Five, the need for financial stability to support the services of HTH.
- Six, external factors such as the sustainability that is weighted heavily in grant applications and the opportunity for social innovation grants also contributed to the development of Operation Grow. The initiative is consistent with the strategic emphasis on evidence-based service.

Operation Grow

Operation Grow is a social enterprise that will provide women survivors with an opportunity to increase resiliency, network, and build community in a supportive environment. The social enterprise will generate income to sustain its social programs from its vertical farm activities. There are two main components of Operation Grow: (i) the vertical farm, and (ii) the space for non-therapeutic support services.

Operation Grow

Features	Benefits
Employment	Employment income, skills, and knowledge transfer
Food options	Access healthy food
Women-only drop-in space	Access to social network and relevant support services
Yoga and meditation programs	Access to non-therapeutic holistic care
Crisis support	Ensure access to non-therapeutic program and employment
Showering and laundry facilities	Access to non-therapeutic care
Access to whole foods at buyers' club prices	Access to healthy food and increased knowledge of nutrition
Community kitchen	Access to healthy food

Operation Grow transcends conventional programs for survivors of sexual violence that are focused on individual or group therapy. It will provide evidence-based support and opportunity that have been proven to reduce the impact of trauma for women. Huronia Transition Homes recognizes that poor and marginalized women face multiple barriers which often compound their experience of trauma and so it is critical that programs focus on reducing barriers for marginalized women.

The Vertical Farm

The vertical farm is central to the goals and outcomes of Operation Grow. Vertical farming is a technology-based farming system in which food/crops are grown in vertically stacked panels in internally controlled environment. This enables the organization to produce food/crops year round production. Vertically farming is innovative and yet to be implemented in Simcoe County.

SWOT Analysis

Strengths	Weaknesses	Opportunity	Threats
• Vertical farming can produce food year round • HTH can deploy a variety of distribution channels such as local restaurants, farmer's markets, and local grocery stores • HTH can adapt pricing strategy of its produce in order to gain competitive advantage • New revenue stream for HTH • Employees and the board are committed to the social enterprise Supported social enterprise advantage	• Lack of employees to train new employees • Start-up costs and continuous funding are not guaranteed • Limited experience in business processes • Limited experience in marketing • Limited experience in financial management	• Employment opportunities for the community • Networking for employees, employers, and the community members • Employees gain desirable employment skills • Modular Farm's unique vertical farming design eliminates competition by not operating additional farms within a 100 km • Opportunity to provide education and awareness to the community about the mission	• Being a new entrant into this market • Limited barrier to entry • The vertical farm will not be profitable for the initial 2 to 3 years • Competition from a potential local vertical farm in close proximity that is using a different technology

Organizational Structure

- The organizational structure of the social enterprise is comprised of: Executive Director; Supervisor, Farm; Supervisor Support Services; Cultivators; Yogis; Building Maintenance; Meditation Instructors; and Volunteers
- The organizational structure should be reviewed to ensure that it supports the goals of the social enterprise.

Organizational Structure

Employee and Volunteer Engagement

HTH is an organization that has grown from a single program that was focused on women's shelter to a multi program and multi site organization. The services of the organization include women who have been sex trafficked, a sexual assault counselling and advocacy centre, a children's program for children exposed to abuse against their mothers. The Operation Grown social enterprise is a unique opportunity to leverage the mission and value proposition to better serve and empower the women. To achieve this objective, HTH, must engage employees and volunteers.

Discussion Questions

1. Is it necessary for Kathy Willis to be concerned about employee and volunteer engagement?
2. How would you suggest that HTH should go about developing the engagement plan?
3. Which of the engagement models in this book is relevant to HTH?
4. What are some of the challenges that you envisage that HTH will encounter when developing and implementing an engagement plan?
5. What strategy would you recommend that Kathy Willis should implement to address the challenges?

Index

A
Ability-motivation-opportunity (AMO), 107, 134
Accidents, 27, 65, 100, 187
Accountability, 45–47, 166
Adequate resources, 20
Advocacy, 41, 48, 58, 61, 142, 157–159, 161, 162, 164–169, 197
Affect, 16, 25, 28, 41, 45, 46, 62, 64, 66, 87, 103, 127, 141, 143, 144, 148, 150, 158, 167, 177, 182
Akingbola, K., 51, 59, 60, 62–67, 83–90
Akingbola & van den Berg's Model of Antecedents and Consequences with organization and job engagement mediators, 84
Analytic Methods for Measuring Employee Engagement, 187
Antecedents, 13, 15, 18, 19, 21, 22, 29, 43, 59, 63, 64, 66–68, 77, 82–84, 86, 89–91, 175, 186, 187
Assessment of Employee Engagement into Everyday Practice, 183
Autonomy, 14, 15, 18, 20, 28, 81, 87, 127–130, 145, 179

B
Barriers to advocacy, 168
Behaviors, 1–4, 7–12, 14, 16, 18, 21, 24, 26–30, 51, 54, 61, 62, 66, 67, 80, 81, 87
Board of directors, 30, 50, 56, 61, 141–147, 149–154, 157, 162, 192, 194
Board's involvement, 142
Burnout, 4, 24, 65, 79, 81, 97–100, 104, 151

C
Career opportunities, 19
Caring human resources management, 99
Change, 26, 28, 37, 38, 40, 41, 44, 46, 48, 50, 51, 53, 55, 56, 102,

103, 112, 120, 132, 151, 158, 161, 167, 168, 182, 184, 187
Commitment, 4, 11, 13, 14, 17, 21, 39, 51–54, 58, 60, 65, 66, 79, 81, 89, 90, 102, 113, 124, 125, 129, 143, 144, 149, 153, 173, 174, 181, 184, 188, 192
Commitment and Loyalty, 181
Communication and implementation, 22
Community needs, 43, 50, 58, 60, 67
Competition, 47, 133, 161, 196
Constructive volunteer-employee relations, 125, 131, 133, 136
Continuous development, 124, 130
Continuum of Involvement, 146
Counterproductive workplace behaviors (CWBs), 174, 183
COVID-19, 44, 45, 46, 48, 77, 78, 102
Customer satisfaction, 18, 27, 65

D
Discretionary effort, 5, 10, 26, 59, 61, 81, 179, 182, 188
Disengagement, 28, 95, 97, 100, 104, 134
Donative labor hypothesis, 53

E
Economy, 43–45, 47
Ecosystem, 142, 143, 147, 148, 150, 151, 153, 161, 181
Emotional contagion, 16, 28
Emotions, 3, 5, 7, 8, 10–12, 14, 16, 18, 20, 24–26, 29, 58–61, 63–65, 67, 79, 80, 95, 96, 106, 112, 121, 122, 136, 175, 181, 191
Employee antecedents, 18, 19, 22

Employee engagement: team and collective organizational engagement definitions, 8
Employee engagement: What is it for organizations., 24
Employee health and wellness, 97, 98, 101, 110, 113
Employee participation, 20
Employee productivity and performance, 174, 180
Employee volunteer partnership, 53
Empowerment, 19, 154
Enhanced work design, 124, 126
Equity, 19, 108, 127, 144, 148, 152, 153, 165
Equity and fairness, 19, 28
Expressive function, 55
Extrinsic rewards, 52, 62

F
Flexible work arrangement, 97, 98, 102–104, 111, 113
"Free-Range" Board, 142, 143
Funding, 45–47, 50, 53–56, 61, 67, 89, 161, 196
Funding engagement, 55

G
Governance engagement, 55

H
Helicopter board, 145, 147
Human resource management, 3, 8, 29, 49, 63, 67, 96, 97, 100, 106, 107, 134
Huronia Transition Homes (HTH), 191, 192, 194–197

INDEX

I
Innovation, 26, 67, 106, 112, 158, 159, 164, 165, 173, 194
Innovative work behavior, 67
Instrumental function, 55
Integrated Nonprofit Employee Engagement Model, 86
Intention to quit, 62, 66, 67, 84, 90, 179
Intrinsic, 6, 14, 23, 24, 52, 62, 63, 80, 81
Intrinsic motivation, 14, 52, 53, 62, 63, 68, 87, 88

J
Job characteristics, 10, 62, 84, 97, 103, 179
Job Characteristics Model (JCM), 127–130
Job Characteristics Theory, 128
Job Demand-Resources (JD-R), 14, 78, 80–83, 85, 86, 91, 97, 98
Job demands, 15, 61, 62, 80–82, 88, 97–99, 104, 113
Job design, 8, 16, 20, 21
Job engagement, 7, 79, 80, 83, 84, 97, 113, 179
Job resources, 11, 14, 15, 17, 20–22, 24, 28, 43, 80–82, 86, 87, 97–99, 109, 175, 187
Job satisfaction, 13, 25, 62, 64, 84, 89, 96, 100, 110, 174, 175, 179

L
Leaders, 21, 22, 96–99, 103–113, 120, 124–127, 129–134, 136, 160, 174, 179–188
Leadership, 8, 15, 16, 20–22, 25, 50, 53, 67, 86, 87, 97–99, 106, 108, 110, 112, 113, 124, 137, 141, 143, 146, 148, 160, 162, 175, 191
Leadership antecedents, 18, 21, 22
Lobbying, 157–159

M
Management engagement, 56
Meaningfulness, 7, 9, 10, 17, 20, 21, 23, 28, 30, 60, 62, 64, 65, 85, 177, 178, 180
Mission, 2, 7, 18, 30, 37–43, 45, 47, 48, 50–67, 89, 91, 125, 133, 144, 153, 157, 159, 160, 165, 173, 179–181, 192, 196, 197
Mission attachment, 59, 68, 84, 85, 87, 88
Model, 1, 14, 21, 29, 30, 77, 78, 80–87, 91, 97–99, 107, 112, 134, 150, 151
Motivation, 4, 11, 12, 14, 17, 52, 54, 58, 59, 62, 67, 81, 88, 97, 98, 105–107, 121, 129, 136, 162, 173
Motivational mechanism, 12, 17
Multidimensional approach, 7, 79, 80, 83, 84

N
Nonprofit mission engagement, 54

O
Operation Grow, 191, 192, 194, 195, 197
Organizational antecedents, 18, 19, 21, 22
Organizational citizenship, 26
Organizational citizenship behaviors (OCBs), 62, 66, 81, 84, 90, 96, 174, 179, 182, 183

Organizational commitment, 9, 62, 65, 96, 110, 179–181
Organizational engagement, 7, 9, 120, 179, 184
Organizational fairness perceptions and trust in senior leadership, 107
Organizational identification, 174, 181
Organizational impacts definitions, 5
Organizational learning, 125, 130

P
Perceptions of trust in the organization, 19
Performance management, 30, 105, 107, 111, 124, 126, 130, 187
Performance standards, 46, 47, 105
Physical, cognitive, and emotional energy, 95
Political advocacy, 41, 158
Problem solver, 21
Productivity, 6, 25, 65, 96, 103, 109, 111, 173, 175, 180, 187, 188
Profit, 25, 52
Psychological Explanations for Volunteerism, 120
Psychological meaningfulness, 21, 23
Psychological state, 5, 9, 13, 17, 22, 26, 28, 127
Public service motivation, 52, 59, 60, 65, 82, 87–89

Q
Qualitative Methods, 186
Quality of work life, 23, 24

R
Recognition and rewards, 125, 135
Rewards and recognition, 19, 62, 84

Role clarity, 97, 98, 104, 105, 111, 113

S
Safety, 20, 22, 23, 27, 60, 62, 96, 106, 112, 177, 178, 187
Satisfaction, 11–13, 17, 23, 66, 100, 102, 127, 129, 130, 135, 143, 145, 152, 173, 179–181, 184, 188
Selander's Work Engagement, 82
Service delivery engagement, 55
Services, 27, 28, 38–41, 43–48, 50, 51, 53–57, 60, 63, 67, 78, 88, 90, 91, 96, 100, 101, 104, 106, 110, 112, 119, 124, 130, 131, 135, 142, 147, 150, 153, 158, 160, 161, 164, 173, 187, 192–195, 197
Shared values (value congruence), 11, 15–17, 21, 39, 43, 60, 88
Social capital, 37, 41, 51, 56
Social change, 41, 48, 158, 161, 166, 191
Social enterprise, 41, 191–194, 196, 197
Social Exchange theory, 78–80, 83, 85, 86, 91
Sociological and Other Academic Explanations for Volunteerism, 121
Strategic board, 149–154
Supervisor and coworker support, 106, 107
Survey-Based Methods, 184

T
Teamwork experience, 19
Technology, 47, 48, 167, 168, 196
Three Approaches to Involvement, 147

Transformational leadership, 21, 22, 87, 112
Turnover, 16, 25, 26, 65–67, 90, 95, 100, 103, 110, 111, 125, 127, 129, 146, 151, 180, 186–188
Turnover rates and intention to stay, 174

V

Value alignment, 124, 126
Value-based resources, 88
Value congruence, 60, 82–85, 88, 89, 177, 178
Values, 2, 7–9, 15–17, 19, 21, 22, 37, 39, 40, 43, 46, 50–56, 60–66, 79, 88–90, 103, 109, 121, 124–126, 133, 136, 147, 178, 179, 181, 186, 192, 193, 197
van Den Berg, H.A., 51, 59, 60, 62–67, 83–90
Vision and shared values, 21
Volunteer engagement, 119, 120, 124, 126, 127, 129, 130, 132–134, 136, 137, 192
Volunteers, 30, 37–40, 43, 47, 50, 51, 53–57, 61, 91, 119–136, 149, 152–154, 162, 173, 191, 192, 196, 197

W

Well-being, 5, 14, 20, 23, 24, 64, 66, 80, 81, 99–101, 110, 143, 178
Workforce engagement, 100, 105, 109, 187
Work-life balance, 97–100, 103, 109, 110, 113
Work role definitions, 4

Printed in the United States
by Baker & Taylor Publisher Services